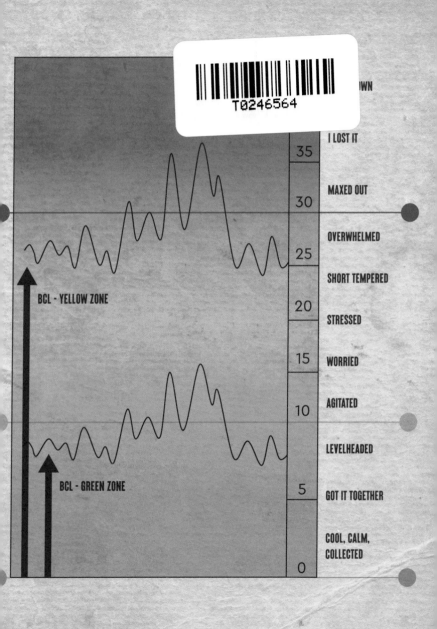

Praise for *TAKE THE WHEEL*

"*Take the Wheel* helped me make a positive change in my life, reinforced my gut intuition, and gave me total confidence on this new path headed toward my goals."

–DEDRICK W., veteran, VA employee,
and veterans' advocate

"This book helped break my habit of worry by teaching me to watch my thoughts as the observer, giving me flexibility and quiet in my mind again. Thank you."

–POPPY W., LMT (licensed massage therapist)

"The red zone, yellow zone, green zone really resonated and just clicked. Just letting my brain slow allowed me to sleep and get out of the constant red zone. That let me work on what was causing it."

–ERIC S., computer engineer

"This is the book I keep coming back to. Especially with my super-stressful, upper yellow zone lifestyle. I now know how to meditate in action and stay calm and focused."

–GREG H., Lieutenant, Los Angeles Police Department

"Our mental healthcare system must head toward the self-awareness, self-knowledge, and self-experience so clearly explained in this curative guide."

—KRISTEN R., PMHNP (psychiatric mental health nurse practitioner)

"I hit a wall in life and a literal wall on the trail, and I learned how to overcome both."

—DUSTIN D., entrepreneur and former corporate executive

"I took away from this book invaluable insights about mental wellness and relinquishing the pursuit of control, improving my approach to life."

—JILL S., PhD in biomedical sciences

"I've read a lot of books over the years, and this is one of the very few to become a dog-eared guide."

—BILL L., retiring manufacturing executive

"Be authentic. Lose the ego. Stay present. Face the emotions. Avoid the red zone. It's all in here."

—SHAMAN STEVE

"This book is a testament to two men who embraced their darkness and found their path to peace."

—DONA N., LMFT (licensed marital family therapist), former 911 dispatcher

TAKE THE WHEEL

Published by Wonderwell Press

Austin, Texas
www.gbgpress.com

Distributed by Greenleaf Book Group

For ordering information or special discounts for bulk purchases, please contact Greenleaf Book Group at PO Box 91869, Austin, TX 78709, 512.891.6100.

Design and composition by Greenleaf Book Group
Cover design by Adrian Morgan

Publisher's Cataloging-in-Publication data is available.

Print ISBN: 978-1-963827-02-6

eBook ISBN: 978-1-963827-03-3

To offset the number of trees consumed in the printing of our books, Greenleaf donates a portion of the proceeds from each printing to the Arbor Day Foundation. Greenleaf Book Group has replaced over 50,000 trees since 2007.

Printed in the United States of America on acid-free paper

24 25 26 27 28 29 30 31   10 9 8 7 6 5 4 3 2 1

First Edition

TAKE THE WHEEL

An Offroad Monks Guide
to Quiet Your Mind
and Get Back in the
Driver's Seat of Life

bryan bernard & tommy stoffel

WONDERWELL

CONTENTS

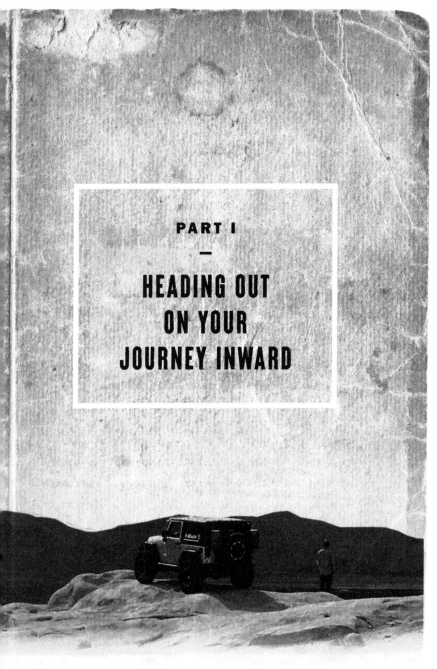

PART I
—
HEADING OUT ON YOUR JOURNEY INWARD

CHAPTER 1

THE NOISE IN YOUR HEAD
- Dust on the Trail -

When it comes to friends, the voice in your head is rarely one of them. —*A Fortune Cookie*

D O YOU LIKE UNSOLICITED ADVICE? Most people don't. Yet, there is no shortage of friends, strangers, leaders, books, and videos that want to tell you how to behave and what to think. "Simply do *this* and you will be happy." That's not what this book is about. Because rarely, when dealing with internal and fundamental life-force issues, is someone else's answer *your* answer.

We aren't here to give you our answers to happiness or inner peace. But what we can do is help you quiet the noise in your head so that you can hear your own answers to what matters to you and who you want to be in this life.

What is the noise in your head?

We call it chatter.

Chatter is the never-ending dialogue running in your head. It's the constant stream of thoughts that bounce around from one topic to the next with lightning speed. It's that voice in your mind that we all have, the one you're always talking to or listening to (or telling to shut up). It's the continuous roller coaster of worries about the future and the never-ending rehashing of the past. It never stops. And with certainty, yours is going right now. Your head is full of chatter at this very moment.

Your chatter is like dust on the trail. It's the hazy cloud you kick up while off-roading that never seems to dissipate. It's in your way. Your chatter, just like that dust, is what makes it nearly impossible to see a path forward and to know where you are.

As you'll soon learn, a large percentage of your thoughts are repeat worries, anxieties, and fears. They seem almost hardwired and automatic. They are unhelpful thoughts, mountain-out-of-a-molehill thoughts, and never-ending thought loops. Having less of that type of chatter will clear space in your mind and bring a quiet calm you may not have felt in a long time.

We've learned, through firsthand experience and through

the hundreds of people that have joined us on our Offroad Monks® adventures, that when the noise takes control, our life can easily become a life we don't recognize as our own. Slowly, incrementally, bit by bit and year after year, we inch away from the life our true selves wanted to experience and into a life we "should" be living. Sometimes we march along, performing and behaving as friends, family, and society expects, without noticing the disparity, until one day we look up and realize we are far removed from where we wanted to go and who we wanted to be.

We have taken our hands off the wheel and are very deep inside a life not entirely of our choosing.

Since you're reading this book, there's a high probability some (or many) things in your life aren't going the way you'd like. Maybe you know exactly what they are. Maybe all you know is that you have this vague, nagging feeling that something isn't right, but you can't quite put your finger on it. Maybe it's your relationships. Maybe it's your work. Maybe it's a dozen things. And maybe it's you.

Sometimes a little adjustment or a bandage here and there can straighten you right out. But then there are the times you may feel like you've "had it up to here" or like you just can't take any more. Sometimes you feel that you are so far off the trail, like we were, that you find yourself on the edge of breaking down, like we actually did.

This book is your trail guide back to your true self, back into the driver's seat of your life. It is a bridge to help you get over your obstacles faster and easier, so you don't have to walk through the mud all by yourself, and you won't need to suffer for years not knowing why the same problems keep cropping up for you.

Over the years we've been blessed, as the Offroad Monks, to take groups of people on fun-filled off-roading adventures we call Soul Outings, where we help them overcome obstacles on the trail and obstacles in their lives. People show up with all kinds of obstacles in their path, like extreme stress, overwhelming worry, broken relationships, unresolved trauma, and much more. During an adventure with us, where we take them deep into the remote peace and beauty of nature, we help them climb over those obstacles—we help them conquer the noise in their heads.

Together we will take you on a similar journey into the wilderness of your own mind. You will hit the trail, by figuring out where you want to go and what changes you wish to make in your life. You'll learn to navigate rugged terrain and create a road map to a quieter mind and the life you've been seeking, and last—if you choose—you will brave the wilderness of your mind and experience the real-life changes that will land you at your destination.

WE WEREN'T ALWAYS OFFROAD MONKS
Tommy's Journey

In 2005, I woke up in a hospital bed next to a man who had tried to commit suicide overnight. How I ended up here is a long and winding story which began when my dog, who was my best friend and source of unconditional love in my life, was killed by a school bus when I was eleven. That tragedy caused a very young Tommy to shut down his heart, swearing never to feel that pain again. I spent the next thirty years bottling up and shutting down all my emotions until my system could no longer take the internal pressure.

I allowed my mind to run all aspects of my life with few feelings involved or considered. Everything was thought-based, and my mind became exceedingly good at churning and racing and overwhelming me with worry and stress and trying to control everything, all while keeping my emotions suppressed. The only thing I found to shut my damn mind off was copious amounts of alcohol, which only made things worse. The pressure kept building, and I was increasingly making one bad decision after another. All the thoughts in my head had somehow become my worst enemy. And then one day I snapped. I actually ran away from home at forty-something, only to come crawling back home the next day, mumbling, "My brain isn't working right" and calling 911.

That's how I woke up in the psychiatric ward next to a sleeping man strapped to his bed. While he slept, I asked the wall, "What the fuck am I doing here?" My mind instantly answered back, "You are here to learn." I wasn't sure exactly where this answer was coming from, but I knew this "voice" came from within me, that it was not an external voice, and that it came from a place of knowing, familiarity, and authority, and it wasn't kidding around. I knew it was a wiser part of me that usually wasn't as direct or forceful as it was that day. It was accompanied by an overwhelming sense of knowing that was more feeling than thought. This was a true and powerful aha moment. "You are here to learn what happens inside the mind of a human being that pushes them to the edge and lands them here."

I knew this voice wasn't to be trifled with, so I agreed, "School's in session." I then asked, "What's the difference between me and what's in my head, compared to some-one free to stroll by the hospital on the sidewalk right now and what's in their head?" I was staring at the blank hospital room wall and the answer came as an image of a green-yellow-red chart appearing on the wall, almost like a slide projection on a screen, the menacing bright red at the top of the chart showing how high the level of noise in my head had gotten. It was very clear. This was the solution to the problem that had put both me and my roommate in a guarded hospital room. This was the splinter in my mind. This is what was driving me mad. When the young man in the bed next to me woke up, we talked at length. I was free to sit up, but he was bound to the bed by thick leather straps, his wrists bandaged underneath, just like you see in the movies. His story was of a man doing his best, trying to succeed, trying to provide for his family, and he became so overwhelmed by the relentless barrage of worries, fears, and expectations that he arrived at the singular point where the only solution he could see was death.

I spent the next two weeks talking with, and learning from, each patient. Everyone wanted to talk. Everyone had a story. A common thread emerged: The voices in people's heads can be so busy with worries and memories and to-dos and have-tos that it doesn't take much to push them over the edge. I got repeated confirmation that the level of noise in people's heads had a direct correlation to someone reaching the breaking point. I also learned, together with everyone else, that it was a decidedly bad idea to tell the psychiatrist you had voices in your head. That only led to more medication. This woke me up, too. We all have voices in our heads. The only solution is to medicate? There had to be a better way.

I had been busy working hard to attain everything society said I should have to be happy. I was living in a nice house, with a nice family, with a nice car, and *nice* credit card bills. I was also living high in what I would come to call the yellow zone of chatter, and it didn't take much to push me into the red zone, into the breaking point. The chart I saw on the wall that day was a key to measuring the noise in my head, to making sure I didn't end up in that hospital bed again. I knew then and there that I had to share it.

———

Bryan's Journey

I hit rock bottom in 2019 at the top of a mountain with a loaded 9 mm handgun pressed against my temple and my finger on the trigger. Milliseconds from death. I had "everything," as any outsider would have judged my life, but I was miserable. I didn't like my life. I didn't like who I'd become.

When the second of my two sons moved out of the house after college, I realized one of my primary identities in life, that of a father, was over. Yes, I will always be their dad, but at this stage of their lives they don't need you as much. Not like when they were little, or in school, or even in the college years (when "Dad" was frequently spelled "ATM"). A huge chunk of me was gone. This event spurred me to look around at other areas of my life, and I did not like what I saw. I was not happy in my marriage. I hated the work I spent too many hours doing. I had no close friends. I had no hobbies. I'd been so busy running on the treadmill of life and chasing success that I'd failed to lift my head and look around at who I was and where I was going and whether I was okay with any of it. And now that I had, I did not like what I saw. I'd succeeded in winning the rat race, but I had become a rat. Now what?

I was overwhelmed with the stress, pressure, and dissatisfaction from work, my marriage, and myself. Worry was my best friend. I felt trapped. I had obligations to many others. I had responsibility for many more. I'd managed to keep all the plates spinning for years, but I was breaking down and plates were beginning to crash to the ground.

I sold my business, left my marriage, and moved into a tiny studio apartment. My entire life—one I'd spent decades building—was gone. My entire persona, one I'd spent decades fortifying, was someone I didn't recognize and no longer wanted to be. I'd gained the world and lost my soul. I didn't know what to do. I didn't know who I was. I was mired in a deep depression, and trying to hide that depression from others was becoming increasingly difficult. I'd tried just about every Western talk therapy there is, but none of it worked for me. I think I was too far gone at that point.

I set down the gun just to see if anyone cared enough to check on me. Much to my surprise, I had cell service *and* I had a voicemail from Tommy. I'd met Tommy about a year prior and thankfully he never gave up on me, even though I had. He spent a couple hours on the phone with me and helped me away from the edge. He said we still had a lot of Jeeping to do and that he knew a few things that would help me.

We subsequently spent many hours together, Jeeping all over the place, having fun, and overcoming obstacles. Tommy shared what he'd learned both in life and from various teachers. It all made such simple sense to me. I learned the source of much of my stress wasn't really the outside sources I thought it was and that I had much more control over what went on between my ears than I thought. I began to understand my endless worries and how to differentiate them from concerns. When I embodied the ideas into my life in practical and tangible ways, they *worked*, and things improved dramatically. Our talks and the implementation of those practices were the beginnings of the book you now hold in your hands.

Over the years, we scoured thousands of pages of books and hundreds of hours of workshops and videos to find the quickest, most effective way of getting out of hell. We did a ton of therapy, both traditional and unconventional. We pulled together everything we learned from sages past and present and what worked for us from all the various sources, distilled it down, simplified it, and lived it. We then began sharing it with others in our Soul Outings. We share it with you now within these pages.

We offer an Experience in each chapter that will help you apply these teachings in your own life. These are exercises to help *you*, with *your* stuff. Do the exercises, have the Experiences. Don't cheat yourself. You'll be reflecting on and writing some deep, personal things in these exercises. You can write them on paper or type them electronically—whatever you prefer—just write about them openly and freely, without holding back. This might mean you need to take steps to make sure no one else ever reads them. Take those steps. Burn the paper or lock it away. Password protect the document. Do whatever it takes for you to feel free to write from your heart. Do not limit yourself and do not edit yourself.

The Experiences in this book will allow you an opportunity, perhaps for the first time ever, to see the noise in your mind written down. You'll be able to read instead of only hearing the voice in your head. This seemingly simple step begins the process of externalizing your worry, fear, and pain. It helps separate *you* from *the thoughts, from the voice,* and facilitates seeing them objectively, for what they might really be and mean. Do not discount the Experiences. Do them with purpose and intention. Remember, if you don't do the work and deal with your stuff, it's just going to keep coming back around.

UNDERSTANDING THE NOISE IN YOUR MIND

The same green-yellow-red chart, or what he would soon come to call the Chatter Level Chart, that Tommy saw on the hospital wall that day many years ago became the foundation for our outdoor adventures and what has helped so many others to understand the level of noise in their heads. There is the *green zone*, where you are pretty calm and peaceful and everything's okay. Then there's a *yellow zone*, where there's some agitation, there's worry, there's stress. And then there's the *red zone*, which is where you are overwhelmed. Most of us are walking around in the yellow zone, where in the back of our heads there's anxiety about something, or there's worry about something else, or there's some underlying pressures and stresses and too much "stuff" going on.

The Chatter Level Chart allows you to visually see how much noise you have in your head. At the end of this chapter, you will have the opportunity to take a stress survey and see where you land on this chart. Wherever on the chart you spend most of your time is your baseline chatter level. *That's* how much noise is in your head. Why is this baseline so important?

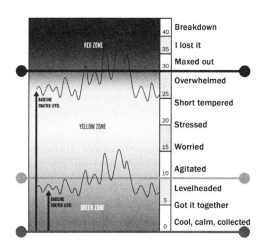

Chatter Level Chart

Let's say your baseline chatter level is in the upper half of the yellow zone. You wake up in the morning and check the news, which is almost always negative, and you also see that you have new messages and emails, some of which are urgent. So, first thing in the morning you've already had a spike in your thinking and you've already gone farther up the chart toward the red zone. Now you head off to work and there is traffic or somebody cuts you off. Another spike. That's the squiggly line on the chart, showing how your noise level fluctuates. As you go through your day it may go up and down, or it may go steadily up—a lot. And that might be okay if your baseline is pretty low, perhaps down in the green zone. But if you are already high in the yellow zone it doesn't take much to push you into the red zone, and that's when you have trouble. That's when you can snap, and react in a harsh or angry way, or lash out at others disproportionately. It's possible to get by in the yellow zone, but when you get in the red zone, you're much more likely to lose control. That's when you might find yourself laying on your horn at other drivers, or yelling at your partner or coworkers, or taking your frustrations out on an innocent child or pet. Living in the red zone makes for a high-stress life, and the amount of stress in your life is directly related to the amount of chatter in your head.

You're likely familiar with the expression "I've had it up to here!" That's how many of us tend to go through life, and when we bounce up into the red zone and snap, we react rather than respond, and we usually regret it later. So, the goal is to lower your baseline chatter level that has built up over time. When the baseline is lowered, you have more room for the inevitable spikes that will occur in life.

This isn't about removing the sources of the spikes from your life—you normally don't have much control over those. Rather, it's about creating space in your head so that when you encounter these spikes, you aren't already so close to, or in, the red zone that you blow a gasket. By lowering your baseline, you'll have a little more clearance in your day to handle the ups and downs and you may not be pushed up into the red zone anymore. Wouldn't that be a good thing for you and those around you?

This book is designed to help reduce that baseline. It can't stop the person that's going to cut you off tomorrow. It can't change the boss who's a pain in the butt. It can't stop the battery from dying in your car. It can't remove the squiggly line on the chart. That squiggly line is your life. But it can help you understand what makes up that noise in the first place. That way the next time something happens in life, something that would normally set you off, you'll be aware of what's going on. You'll be able to say, "You know what? I know what that is now. It's just more noise. I'm not going to allow my mind to run away at full speed and drag me with it. I'm going to stop before it gets going." With a little navigational assistance, you'll be able to decide for yourself what is noise and mostly a waste of time, and what isn't noise and therefore might be worth taking on. And, even better, you'll learn how to diminish the noise that will invariably come your way in life.

This book is here to help you reduce the unwanted noise between your ears. Who defines "unwanted"? *You* do. We will help you get clarity on your chatter so *you* can decide which parts are worth keeping, and which parts you might be ready to let go of.

But first, you need to know your starting point.

Your Chatter Score

The following Perceived Stress Survey will give you your own personal Chatter Score and help you assess your current level of stress.

If taking a simple ten question quiz so soon into your

journey feels daunting to you, think of it like the first scratch on a new car. The anticipation of that first mark is always much worse than the scratch itself. When it inevitably comes, there is always a sense of relief—it's never as bad as you imagined it would be. Identifying your baseline chatter level will be invaluable to lowering it, so muster your courage to *honestly* answer the ten questions that follow.

Sometimes, just knowing your score may give you some measure of relief. If this happens, it's some simple proof that your chatter can be lowered simply by removing the unknown component when your mind is wondering "How bad is it?" Sometimes, this simple awareness alone can lower your chatter level.

Getting your Chatter Score at the beginning of this journey will help you gauge your baseline chatter level and serve as a comparison benchmark when you complete the survey again in the future. Complete this self-assessment periodically in the months after you've finished reading this book as a way to check in with yourself and see how you are progressing.

Each time you complete the survey, place your Chatter Score on the baseline Chatter Level Chart that follows the survey so you can visually track your progress over time.

Keep in Mind:

- When taking the survey for the first time, answer the questions according to how often you felt or thought a certain way *during the last month*.

- Complete the survey again after finishing the book. Answer the questions to indicate how you feel or think *at that time*.

- Don't overthink your answers. Don't dwell on your response. Go with your gut.

Disclaimer: *Your self-assessment and score on the Perceived Stress Survey do not reflect any diagnosis or course of treatment. It is simply meant as a tool to help you assess your own level of chatter and stress, as determined by you. You should consult your doctor or other medical or mental health professional if you have any questions or concerns.*

Perceived Stress Survey

Ignore the score column for now. Answer each question with one of these numbers:

---

0 = Never | 1 = Almost Never | 2 = Sometimes | 3 = Fairly Often | 4 = Very Often

---

	QUESTION	ANSWER	SCORE
1	How often have you been upset because of something that happened unexpectedly?		
2	How often have you felt that you were unable to control the important things in your life?		
3	How often have you felt nervous or stressed?		
4	How often have you felt confident about your ability to handle your personal problems?		
5	How often have you felt that things were going your way?		
6	How often have you found that you could not cope with all the things that you had to do?		
7	How often have you been able to control irritations in your life?		
8	How often have you felt that you were on top of things?		
9	How often have you been angered because of things that were outside of your control?		
10	How often have you felt difficulties were piling up so high that you could not overcome them?		
		Total Score:	

The Perceived Stress Scale[1] is reprinted with permission.

1 Sheldon Cohen, Tom Kamarck, and Robin Mermelstein, "A Global Measure of Perceived Stress," *Journal of Health and Social Behavior* 24, no. 4 (1983): 385–396, https://doi.org/10.2307/2136404.

Go to www.offroadmonks.com/stress-survey or scan the QR code below to take the survey and have it scored online.

How to Score the Perceived Stress Survey:

For questions 1, 2, 3, 6, 9, and 10, your score is the same as your answer. For example, if you answered with a 2, "Sometimes," then your score for that question is also 2.

Score the four remaining questions, 4, 5, 7, and 8, by reversing your answer like this:

Answer	Score
0	4
1	3
2	2
3	1
4	0

Enter your score next to each question and add all ten up to get your total score. Total scores range from 0 to 40. Place your total scores on the following Chatter Level Chart.

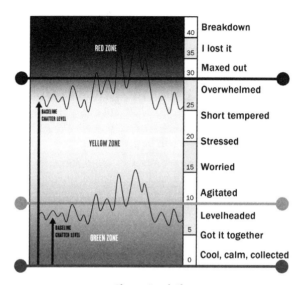

Chatter Level Chart

CHAPTER 2

THE ASK
– Guys *Can* Ask for Directions –

The answers will be given to those
who are bold enough to ask. —*Amit Kalantri*

LET'S RETURN TO THE ORIGINAL QUESTION: Do you like unsolicited advice? Do you ever ask for directions? You're probably familiar with the stereotype of guys not asking for directions, but as with most stereotypes, it's not true 100 percent of the time for 100 percent of guys. The good news is, whether it applies to you or not, we are not here to tell you where to go and what roads to take. Instead, this chapter is about allowing yourself to ask for guidance on your journey—and the person you are going to stop to ask for directions is *you*.

When you understand how to quiet the never-ending

stream of thoughts in your head, you'll be able, perhaps for the first time in your life, to ask *your own questions* about who you are, what you want, where you want to go, and how you want to be in your life. More importantly, within this inner quiet, you'll hear *your own answers*.

So often we go through life without pausing to ask ourselves exactly what we want, or we ask, but don't have the mental silence to hear the answer. We begin our metaphorical journey with the Ask to help you remember that it's okay to ask yourself for a change and that you have the power to improve your life. We start here to help return your confidence in your ability to make your life better, to help you understand that you *can* help yourself. Think of your Ask as a key to unlock the door of your off-road vehicle before you begin this journey. You have to freely ask to open the door to your inner world—no external coercion, no unsolicited advice.

You may be familiar with the phrases, "Ask, and you shall receive. Seek, and you shall find. Knock, and it shall be opened." Put your Ask out into your life and you will receive answers. Here's a little proof: In some way, perhaps small, perhaps subconsciously, you must have already asked for something . . . help, guidance, a nudge in a different direction . . . because you picked up this book. You asked, you found, and you knocked when you opened this book.

Perhaps you already know what you'd like to ask for in yourself or your life and therefore already know your Ask. But if not, here is some guidance on how you might determine your Ask. First, do not feel pressure to get your Ask "right" right away.

Second, you are going to ask for some things for yourself, which many guys don't take time to ever do. This isn't an Ask for material items or gains. This is an Ask for something that will make your life better. You can ask for anything and you can change your mind anytime and ask for something different. What you ask for isn't important to us. What matters is that you ask for something *you* want.

Unless you truly want unsolicited advice, this is your opportunity to ask for what you want, voluntarily and purposefully. You need to ask for help. You need to ask for directions. They can't be forced on you.

THE ASK

In a moment, we are going to prompt you to make your Ask, but before you do, there is something you should understand. Once you've settled on something you want to ask for, you have to *really* ask. Genuinely and from the depths of your being, ask for what *you* want. Don't just lazily toss it out there in passing. You're not asking for a trinket; you're asking for something that *really matters to you,* so ask like it *really matters to you.* Contemplate and reflect on it. Form and mold your thoughts and feelings around it. Focus on *what* you are asking for and not the *how* or the *when.* You have a say in what you ask for, but often you have little to no say in how or when the answer to your Ask will show up, so let those go. Try not to have predefined answers you hope to get in return. Sit quietly and have an honest conversation with yourself and get a feel for what your gut says. And then ask.

Be honest, forthright, and genuine. Don't be ashamed of your Ask. Do not think "Who am I to ask for *that*?" Do not judge it as good or bad. Make it matter to you, not to anybody else. Don't ask for things solely because you think others would approve of them. Be selfish. This is about improving *you* and *your* life, so make it something important to *you.* It should come from your heart, not your head.

Experience: Make Your Ask

Since this is your first Experience in this book, we want to remind you of some important things we said in chapter 1 about these Experiences. You need to write freely and from your heart, whether that is on paper, electronically, or in the margins of this book. Take steps to keep what you write confidential. This is for your eyes only for now. Do not underestimate the value of writing things down. Doing so gets it out of your head, where it lives virtually as a thought, as a voice, and makes it more physical, more real.

As you ponder the following questions and what they mean for you, try not to *think* of answers. Try instead to *feel* what comes up the strongest or the quickest. Trust your gut and don't try to rationalize it. In these important matters of your life, what you feel is going to be more deeply true than what you think. Your mind will probably offer up memorized answers because it's trained to keep track of such things and regurgitate them on demand. This doesn't necessarily mean they aren't true for you, so take note of them, but begin to tune in to how you *feel* by listening to your inner voice and trusting your gut instinct.

To help you determine your Ask, answer these questions:

1. What does the world need more of or less of?
   Write down two or three ideas that immediately
   come to you.

2. What do you think the people close to you need more of or less of in their lives? Maybe it will be some of the same things you wrote for the first question, or maybe something new will come up, but write down the first two or three that pop up.

3. What do *you* need more of or less of in life? This could still be a couple of the same things you've already written about, or they could be completely different, but write down two or three things you strongly feel you want more of or less of in your life.

4. Choose one thing you wrote down for yourself that *really* resonates with you inside. This is your Ask.

Turn Your Ask into an Affirmation

You've now settled on what you are going to ask for to begin your inner expedition. Now you are going to take your Ask one step further by turning it into an affirmation. Forming your Ask as a present moment affirmation makes it far more powerful than a someday-in-the-future possibility. If you leave your Ask out in the future, then it will always be something you can deal with tomorrow, and that tomorrow may never come. You're asking for something *now*, on *this* journey.

Writing your affirmations down makes them more tangible, laying the groundwork for the lived experiences ahead of you. Choose from the phrases below and fill in the blanks with your Ask.

I enjoy having more _____ in my life.

I enjoy having less _____ in my life.

I love life when I have more _____ and less _____.

Life is more fulfilling when _____ happens.

Life is better because _____ doesn't bother me as much.

How often do you actually sit down and ask for something for yourself in writing? It's a powerful experience. Be grateful to yourself and thank yourself for what you just did. Now stop reading and do it again: Be grateful to yourself and thank yourself for what you just did.

The last part of the Ask is paying attention to answers.

Pay Attention to Answers

Once you've asked your Ask, begin paying attention for answers. Too many times too many people are way too busy in their lives and in their heads so when answers are given to them, they completely miss them (and then usually complain that they didn't get any answers). Your answers probably won't announce themselves. They probably won't arrive on a flying unicorn accompanied by blaring trumpets and a neon sign flashing "HERE IS YOUR ANSWER!"

Begin paying attention to the little things in life—things you might not have previously noticed or that you might have dismissed quickly. You need to do this because you do not know in what form answers will be given to you. There could be an incredibly small and easy-to-miss clue that points you in a new direction. That clue might lead to answers to your Ask, but it also might lead you to another clue you need to pay attention to. Picture this as more of a flowing treasure hunt than a rigidly controlled trip with nothing between you and your destination. Because you asked from a deep place within yourself for something that is deeply important to you, your subconscious mind will begin noticing both indirect clues and outright answers.

For example, *listen* when talking to people, *notice* things that are presented to you or cross your path, *hear* song lyrics you've never paused to reflect on, *read* if someone tells you about a book. If you begin paying attention to life, you'll start to recognize things that seem like coincidences.

You'll think, "Wow! That's a coincidence. And that's a coincidence. There's another coincidence!" *The truth is all of these "coincidences" are happening because you've asked for them.* Pay attention!

Now you'll see what happens on your journey. As you begin to pay attention to life around you, you'll be better able to pay attention to answers—*your* answers, to *your* Ask.

CHAPTER 3

THE TURN
- Toward Inner Terrain -

Be the change you wish to see in the world.
—*commonly attributed to Mahatma Gandhi*

I T'S EASY TO LOOK AROUND the world outside of you and see things that you feel should change. Things that need to be fixed over here, others that need to get better over there. If only this or that person or "those people" would think or behave differently then things would be better. And while all that might very well be true, this next step in your journey isn't about pointing fingers at others, but about looking inward. Guided by your Ask—what you want more of or less of in your life—you are now ready to make *the Turn* toward, or away from, some things in yourself and your life.

This is your opportunity to begin to BE in your life differently. All those outside things that you feel should change need to wait while you get your own house in order. To see your outer world reach a state of peace, wisdom, and harmony, first you have to arrive there within.

"Be the change you wish to see in the world" is a quote you may have heard before. We are going to pause and contemplate what this means and how it applies in this book. How do you "be the change"? What does that mean? Be the change means *you* have to change, *inside*. In this chapter you will be making an *internal* turn, informed by your Ask. Your Turn is your decision to make, no one else's. Nothing is mandated. You don't need anyone else's approval. This is your opportunity to make a change *for yourself*.

Change can be hard. In many ways, it seems easier to continue down the paved road rather than venture off onto an unfamiliar dirt one. Change can mean upheaval, for yourself and others. Our brains don't like change—they prefer the known, the predictable, and the familiar, even if it's not what you truly want or what is best for you. Our brains are very good at recognizing patterns in all areas of life, including people, places, and routines, and when the pattern changes, our brains are likely to tell us to stay where we are. It will be easy to overthink this by coming up with a long list of reasons why you should stay exactly where you are and keep doing exactly what you've been doing.

Your mind may throw up all kinds of warning signs like "Rough Road Ahead," "Do Not Enter," or "Road Closed." If you get such a sign, keep going. The whole point here is that we're taking the road less traveled, even if it's bumpy.

So instead of using the word *change*, we are going to say *turn*. By taking the Turn, you begin a shift in the direction you truly wish to head. In your Ask, *you* chose what would make your life better, and now you will turn in that direction.

Your Turn can start small. That's perfectly fine. If you turn a ship at sea just one degree, you'll probably not even notice anything has changed. But many miles later you will absolutely be heading in a very different direction. A small turn can make a huge difference.

The process of starting your Turn involves three steps: awareness, understanding, and experience. Imagine you are driving on a dark, unpaved road. With your lights off you won't get very far, but if you switch on your headlights you can get some *awareness* of what's ahead of you and what the road looks like. You can then look closer at the road and see a big rock to your right, a fallen tree covering half the trail, and some water where the road swerves up ahead. Now you are gaining some *understanding* about the road you are on. Then you step on the gas and steer your wheel and have the *experience* by driving down the road with your new awareness and understanding.

We learn best by doing. The experience is the doing. It seals the understanding of the new thing you became aware of into your being. Where would you be if you only read the student drivers instruction manual and then went straight to your driver's test without ever having experienced driving a car?

Each chapter within this book has these three steps of awareness, understanding, and experience. We help you become aware of something; we help you understand the thing you became aware of, and we give you an opportunity to experience it. Each experience gives you insight into a new way of being that is entirely of your own choosing. They give you courage to try new things that feel right to you. They give you an opportunity to see how powerful it can be when you bring your new awareness and understanding into your life. Writing it down is just the beginning of the experience. It's a little doing but it isn't the end of your doing. Doing it in your life is the grander experience.

Let's talk about awareness, understanding, and experience as they relate to your Turn.

STEP 1: AWARENESS

The first step is awareness of the Turn, or change, you want to make. In the previous chapter, when you made your Ask, you opened the door to begin considering a change and bringing into awareness what you are seeking. By asking your Ask, you are metaphorically shining your headlights on what you want to turn toward or away from. But don't just notice it and then forget it. Stay with that awareness. If you find yourself forgetting what you want to turn toward or away from, then maybe it isn't that important to you and you will want to go deeper to come up with another Ask. If it really matters to you, you will ponder it often and it will stick with you. If the idea won't leave you alone, it's because your subconscious is trying to get you to do something about it. This is good! Heed that feeling!

STEP 2: UNDERSTANDING

While awareness is all about realizations and waking up to what's in front of you, understanding is about knowledge and insight. While your headlights may now offer some clarity about the road ahead, in order to truly shift your life, you need to understand the Turn you want to make. Sometimes life is easier if we simply keep our eyes closed to any questioning of the path we are on. If you've been doing that, it's time to stop. Open your eyes to where you are in life and who you've become. It is no longer time to blindly trudge down the road well traveled. Be honest with yourself about what it is you want to change. Ask yourself questions to better know your desires and what is or has kept you from them. Why do I want to make this internal Turn? Why have I not made it before? How will this help me with my Ask? What happens if I don't make this Turn?

Dig. Dig deep. It's okay to take your time here for some in-depth self-exploration. You may find some troubling things within you. That's okay. They need to be unearthed. If you do find trouble, you don't necessarily have to run from it. Perhaps you are ready to face it. Perhaps it's bothered you for so long, it's time to make a Turn. If what you are pondering keeps coming up, that's a sign it needs attending to.

STEP 3: EXPERIENCE

Once you have awareness and understanding of the Turn you truly wish to make, you are going to do an exercise to commit yourself to it. Your commitment will begin the process of making your Turn a lived experience as you move forward in life. You will confirm that you are ready to make your Turn. Have the willingness and resolve to make this commitment to yourself.

Experience: Committing to Your Turn

The Experience for this chapter, The Turn, is simple. Say out loud *and* write down the following statement.

"I decide, once and for all, to make this turn and change my life for good."

If other, similar words are more powerful to you, use those. Feel free to add details about the Turn you wish to make. Do not minimize the seemingly simple acts of saying this statement out loud and writing it down. Your Turn begins when you make the commitment to yourself. You're making a pact with yourself, a promise that you are going to make your Turn and that you won't turn back. Honor that.

You have more to do, but do this now.

PART II

—

NAVIGATING YOUR RUGGED TERRAIN

CHAPTER 4

MIND CONTROL
- Don't Overthink the Journey -

Silence is to the mind
what sleep is to the body.
—Unknown

NOW THAT YOU'VE DECIDED, and indeed committed to yourself, to go on this journey, this chapter will help you with that well-practiced mind of yours, so you don't overthink your expedition or second-guess your promise to yourself.

What do you think is humankind's biggest addiction? Stop reading for a minute and think about that question. Did you think of something? Several things? Maybe you thought of drinking, smoking, or wanting to be loved and accepted. Those are all big ones, but admittedly it's a bit of a trick question and telling you to *think* about humankind's biggest addiction actually gives us the answer.

Our biggest addiction is . . . thinking. We are *thinkaholics*.

Think about it for a minute—there's an amusing statement—think about how addicted you are to thinking. Your mind is constantly creating thoughts. It never stops (and it's doing it right now). It is a thought-producing machine, and it is very good at it. From the moment you wake up, your mind begins producing thoughts. Your brain snaps on and it starts thinking. And thinking. And it doesn't stop all day long. We think and we think and we think. We're just one nonstop thinking machine from first thing in the morning until we go to bed at night. We do this day after day, week after week, year after year, and we think we can't stop thinking.

But that is simply not true. You *can* control your thoughts. Your mind is a tool over which you have more control than you may realize. This chapter is called Mind Control because here you will learn how to begin having more command over your thoughts, over that never-ending stream of thoughts you crank out every day, every hour, every minute. Mind Control is not about controlling other people's thoughts or other people's minds. It's about looking inside yourself and asking, "Is my mind in my control, or is it running out of control?"

GAPS IN YOUR THINKING

According to research published by Queen's University in Canada in 2020, study participants averaged about six thousand thoughts per day. The research assumed sixteen waking hours in a day, which works out to about three hundred seventy-five thoughts per hour and a little over *six thoughts per minute*.[2] That's a lot of thoughts! Humans have a natural tendency toward negativity bias, which means we think about negative things more frequently than positive ones, so most of those thoughts aren't helping you.[3] At the risk of telling you to think *more*, stop and think about those numbers for a minute. Do you really need all of those thoughts? *All* of them? Or even most of them? Would it not be a good idea to quiet your coconut a bit and give it a rest?

Your thoughts throughout the day come fast, as you know. Good thoughts, bad thoughts, worried-about-the-future thoughts, remembering-the-past thoughts. They are all over the place most of the time. It can feel like many thoughts are coming at once because they come so fast. But the truth

---

2 Julie Tseng and Jordan Poppenk, "Brain Meta-state Transitions Demarcate Thoughts across Task Contexts Exposing the Mental Noise of Trait Neuroticism," *Nature Communications* 11, no. 3480 (July 13, 2020), https://doi.org/10.1038/s41467-020-17255-9.
3 Kendra Cherry, "What Is the Negativity Bias?" VeryWell Mind, https://www.verywellmind.com/negative-bias-4589618.

is that for most people, the never-ending inner dialogue—
that voice that is "speaking" your thoughts in your head—is
sequential, leaping from one thought to the next. The train
of thoughts that your mind voices in your head is actually
"spoken" a single thought at a time. But it creates these one-
at-a-time thoughts very, very fast. It might feel like we are
multitasking and thinking multiple things at one time, but
that's not normally the case. And that sequential voicing of
our thoughts is going to be our access point to Mind Control.

When your thoughts are voiced one at a time, one fin-
ishes before the next one begins. That means there is a gap
between the thoughts voiced in your head. Yes, that gap is
usually infinitesimally small, but it *is* there. Now, if you've
never paid attention to your thoughts before, or if you've
never meditated, or never done anything where you've analyzed the manner in which you think, you've likely never
focused on this gap. But in that gap, in that truth, is one
of the best-kept secrets on the planet. Because the gap is
where you can find a little bit of rest, a little bit of silence,
a little bit of calm.

Chain of Thoughts

We frequently think we need to search outside ourselves for peace of mind or to make that problem go away. Thinking thoughts like "as soon as I pay off those bills, that'll be one less thing to worry about, and then I'll have a little more space in my brain." The truth is we already have the capability of being calm in our mind. We all have this place of peace in us—it's just a matter of finding the gap and tapping into it. In the Experience at the end of this chapter you are going to do just that: You are going to watch your thoughts come and go, and by doing so you'll be able to access the gap you already have and find a little bit of calm in your mind.

FINDING SILENCE

Silence is such a powerful experience, and the truth is there is silence all around us. Most everything is silent. To hear this for yourself, stop reading and listen closely to your surroundings for a few minutes. Listen to every noise and where it is coming from. The sounds you hear are coming from a very small percentage of the people and things around you. Now, notice how many people and objects around you are silent. That's a much bigger number, isn't it? We think life is so busy and noisy. Well, it's not the external noise that makes you think that but the internal noise that is the loudest and the most persistent. Guess which one you have the most control over? That's what we're here to help calm and settle down.

Let's go back to the quote that began this chapter . . . "*Silence is to the mind what sleep is to the body.*" Our minds need to be powered down once in a while, and we need to have those periods of silence. Your mind needs a break just like your body needs rest. When we sleep at night our brains actually do pause the incessant thinking as we go through cycles of dream state and deep sleep state. But the idea of Mind Control is to consciously summon a little peace of mind when you need to during your waking hours.

Peace of mind is the ability to be alone and at ease with your own thoughts anytime, without external input of any kind—TV, the internet, other people, this book, and so on. This ability brings you to a place of peace. It doesn't mean you are absolutely silent in your own head, and it doesn't mean you're not thinking a single thought. It doesn't mean you don't have *some* noise going on in your head. Rather, it's knowing where the noise is coming from, and knowing it's okay to be alone with it. Peace of mind is knowing the noise doesn't need to be running out of control and taking you down rabbit holes and into fear zones you don't want to go to anymore. You get to choose.

Experience: Minding the Mousehole

The Experience for this chapter will help you learn how to observe your thoughts and find the gaps in between them. It may sound impossible, but give it a try, and not just once. You can do this as often as you'd like to help find and lengthen the space between your thoughts.

Mousehole

Imagine a mousehole—the typical mousehole in the baseboard that you saw in cartoons as a kid. Take a few moments to picture that dark mousehole in your mind. Got it? Now, close your eyes and stare at that mousehole in your mind. Watch it closely. As a thought comes to you, imagine it is coming out of the mousehole. Do not try to bring or force thoughts out. Just let your thoughts come freely. Watch them run up the wall and scurry all over the place and then scamper away. Let them go. Then go back to watching that dark mousehole. Every time you bring your attention back to watching the mousehole after a thought comes out and runs around inside your mind, and before the next thought emerges, you've found the gap between thoughts.

Try this exercise for five minutes, with your eyes closed, sitting quietly someplace where you won't be disturbed. Practice this as often as you can. You can extend the duration if you'd like. If your mind is racing and thoughts are coming, that's okay, just take a deep breath or two and go back to watching the mousehole. Watch your thoughts come and go, but always come back to watching the mousehole. If you notice your mind wandering or chasing a thought, bring your attention back to the mousehole. If this is a challenge or feels difficult, don't worry, it will get easier the next time. Have patience and even some fun watching your thoughts. Hopefully you'll find a pause, the gap between thoughts. Maybe your head will be a little quieter (or maybe a lot!). Maybe your thoughts will slow down, or you'll experience a little relief from the constant flowing stream of chatter. Or, maybe your mind was going nuts the whole time. That's okay. Try this exercise again another time.

No matter what happens during the exercise, you've watched your mind. You've watched it crank out thought after thought. That in itself is a level of awareness that can be new and amazing for people. By watching your thoughts you've shifted your attention and become the observer, not just the creator of your thoughts, and perhaps you'll experience firsthand that you can find a little gap between them every once in a while. This is the beginning of gaining control of your thoughts. This is the beginning of Mind Control.

CHAPTER 5

INNER SAGE
– Be Your Own Trail Guide –

*Behind your thoughts and feelings,
there stands a mighty ruler, an unknown
sage whose name is Self. —Friedrich Nietzsche*

HAVE YOU EVER HELD A BAD BABY? There's no such thing as a bad baby. When we come into this life, every one of us comes as this bright little baby with all this glow and all this potential and all this loving, amazing energy flowing out of us. No matter what's gone on in your life, no matter what's happened to cloud that over, that energy is still in you. It's in everybody. The energy you brought with you into this life is not trivial, so don't dismiss or diminish it. It has never occurred previously and it's unique to you. You are a singular being of energy.

Now, maybe you don't believe that. Maybe your inner light is pretty dim these days or perhaps you're in such a dark place that you can't see even a flicker of your own light. This chapter, and indeed the rest of this book, will help you find it. Stick around and give it a try. It *is* there. Want some proof? In the previous chapter, Mind Control, when you looked at the mousehole and watched your thoughts, who was doing the watching? Who was observing the mind? The part of you that is capable of watching your mind is indeed greater than the mind itself.

We call this energy your *Inner Sage*. You can use different words if they feel better for you. Your Higher Self. Your Inner Guru. Your Inner Divinity. Your Inner Trail Guide. Whatever works for you. We will use Inner Sage. A sage is generally a wise person, and it doesn't have a lot of connotations attached to it. Whatever words you use, they all acknowledge the truth that you have inside of you a nugget, a pearl of the original and very unique energy you were born with, and nothing and no one can take it away from you. It's there no matter how on top of the world you are or how run over by a bus you are feeling. It's there whether everyone loves you or you think nobody knows you exist. It's there whether you are a champion at loving yourself or you have a black belt in kicking your own ass.

Your Inner Sage is your inner knowing and wisdom. Your Inner Sage is responsible for that gut feeling, that intuition, when you just *know* something. You feel it. You sense it. Your Inner Sage knows it before your mind even has a chance to think about it. But when that knowing occurs, all the chatter in your head can come crashing down and bury that deeper wisdom before you have a chance to hear it. This chapter will help you rediscover your Inner Sage so you can better pay attention to it. By learning to observe your thoughts as we talked about in Mind Control, you'll be better able to slow, and even halt, the avalanche of noise.

Let's use the metaphor of an off-roading adventure. Your Inner Sage is the driver. Your mind is the backseat driver. The driver has the larger awareness of how to approach different types of obstacles. It knows where the trail is located and has a vision of why you're going there. The backseat driver, your mind, does all the detailed stuff like checking the weather and planning snacks for the trail and finding the gas stations to get there. The other thing the backseat driver does is try to control the way you drive, excessively commenting about every turn and choice you make. Even though your Inner Sage is in the best possible position to determine how to drive the vehicle—to see where the best line is and how to get over the big rocks—after a while you begin to listen to this backseat driver every time it says, "Slow down," or "Turn back" or tells you to do this or that. Before you know it, your backseat driver has taken over the entire adventure.

That's how many of us go through life—with our mind running things, and we aren't in touch very much (or at all) with the driver, our Inner Sage. We've been conditioned to allow our mind to run the show with very little, or zero, input from the Inner Sage. That's completely backward. Our minds are amazing tools, but they aren't the best tool for *everything*. They shouldn't be in charge of so much, so much of the time. Your Inner Sage, once allowed to truly sit in the driver's seat, will absolutely rely on the mind when the mind is the best tool for the task at hand. But the mind doesn't tend to reciprocate, and once in charge it thinks it knows best and wants to *stay* in charge. Now it's time to allow your Inner Sage to resume the role that it's meant to play.

FREEING YOUR INNER SAGE

Let's go back to the baby. Babies are so very present in every moment. They live life as it happens. They aren't burdened yet by a constant chatter in their head. Life is pure; life is simple. They have not yet taken on parental opinions of good and bad, societal expectations of thought and behavior, shoulds and should nots from institutions like school, church, or government. Their Inner Sage, while obviously still very young and new, is not yet clouded over and covered up by the wave of these outside inputs that await them.

These inputs begin at an early age, and the chatter commences. As the baby becomes a child and then a teenager, the wave grows into a tsunami. We take on more and more of what is around us—thoughts, beliefs, and prejudices. Soon we start judging ourselves based on those inputs from outside ourselves—based on those thoughts, beliefs, and prejudices. And soon that voice in our heads gets louder and louder, its growing chatter drowning out our Inner Sage and diminishing its natural role as an important internal influence we should be paying attention to. If this happens, it can be difficult to hear this wise inner voice. We aren't generally taught how to listen to our Inner Sage, how to foster that relationship with that part of ourselves. So, we shut that part down at some point. It happens at different times and for different reasons. Perhaps for some people it doesn't happen at all, and they stay connected with their inner knowing their whole life, but a lot of us get inundated and overwhelmed by the tsunami.

When you lose touch with your Inner Sage and don't know how to foster your natural harmony with it, you lose a part of your true self. This happens when you unknowingly come to believe, and rely too heavily on, outside inputs from others, whether they are true or not. This wholesale adoption can lead to some false beliefs about yourself, and to becoming unknowingly limited and boxed in by those false beliefs. The voice in your head becomes more negative, and the negative self-talk increases, which becomes the false floor of this box. Thoughts that hold you back become the false ceiling. Worries and fears and anxieties are the bars on the windows. And pretty soon this bright being that you are inside is completely boxed in. It's not anybody's fault. We're simply not usually aware this is happening. But now, you have the opportunity to be aware. Say hi to your Inner Sage. It's been there all along and it's been waiting for you.

The good news is that, if you're in a box, it can be opened. When you know what beliefs make up the walls and floors, the ceiling and the bars, you can dismantle the box. You can kick it open, break it down, smash it apart. You can break out of your box.

Experience: Breaking Out of Your Box

To free your Inner Sage, you are going to focus on the thoughts and beliefs which make up your box. First you are going to identify them, then you will question them.

1. Write down a list of beliefs about yourself, internal restrictions or thoughts that hold you back, and negative opinions about yourself. Writing such a list can be daunting. Seeing such a list in black and white can be unsettling. Do it anyway. Unless, of course, you'd rather stay stuck in your box.

2. Sit quietly with your list and ask yourself questions about each item. Ask questions as your Inner Sage might ask them, which means asking less from well-worn memories in your mind and more from your intuitive gut. Ask questions like: Is that *really* true? *All* of it? Is it possible that even *some* of that is false? Do I still want to believe this?

You're not trying to throw overboard everything you believe about yourself. What you're trying to do is uncover how much of your beliefs are *actually* true and how much of them are dead wood that you should let burn off. Keep the beliefs you choose, set aside those that no longer sit right with your Inner Sage. You're likely going to find some semi-truths and stories, or outright lies that have been taught to you or that you have adopted for yourself, and they are just paper walls to your box. Your Inner Sage is in you, and you're going to let that Sage out of the cage.

CHAPTER 6

ENJOY THE VIEW
- Be Present -

Do not dwell in the past, do not dream
of the future, concentrate the mind
on the present moment. —*Buddha*

O N A JOURNEY SUCH AS THIS, when you are driving through unfamiliar terrain and are perhaps hesitant to proceed down dark and dusty roads, it would be easy to turn around, abandon your quest, and go back to the familiar trails that led you to this book in the first place. So it is understandable if you find yourself asking, "Where *am* I?" Questions like that usually come up because your mind is thinking more about where you used to be or where you might be if you keep going, rather than where you are now. As you will see in this chapter, you are always here, and it is always now. You are taking another step on your journey, indeed the only step you *can* take in any given moment—the next step. Pay attention to where you are now by placing your hands on the wheel, your feet on the floor, and your ass in the seat.

Here's another question for you: *What's the most important thing we can do as human beings?* Maybe you've pondered this one already. If not, take a few moments and do so now. It's a pretty open-ended question and there isn't a right or wrong answer. Here's a hint: There's a clue in the question itself.

Perhaps you thought . . . Empathize? Forgive? Be nonjudgmental? Love unconditionally? All those are absolutely good answers, but as a human being, in order to do those and other things to the best of our ability in a way that feels in alignment with our Inner Sage, we have to *be* here. We have to be a human *being*, not a human *doing*. We don't have to always be running around and doing something, and doing something, and doing something else, but sometimes just *being*. Being *present*. Fully present, with your entire self, and yes, this includes your Inner Sage, right here, right now, in this singular moment. Not the last one. Not the next one. *This* moment.

Being in the present is like that moment on the trail when

you round a bend and see the full expanse of a beautiful valley open before you. It's taking the pause commanded by such a moment to fully take in the view. If you've ever had such an experience, you might recall that sense of peace and awe as you were drawn into the full realization of the majesty of the moment. You may have had a feeling of completeness, a sense of perfection perhaps, and the only word you have is "Wow!" You weren't stopping just to take a picture, anxious to move on to the next view for another picture. Your mind was not on last week's regrets or tomorrow's to-do list. In that moment, all you needed was there. It's both calming and moving.

You may have heard the phrase "Be in the now." The *now* is the time to be present. That's what this chapter is about: the element of being present. When you are present in *this* moment, your energy is connected to the energy around you. You feel fully awake and aware of what is happening . . . *now*. This is the place where life is happening because this is the place where you are *now*.

Since you are always *somewhere*, and it is always *now*, what pulls you away from *now*? What takes you out of this moment? What takes you from *now* to . . . *then*?

Then is both the past and the future. *Then* is not *now*.

We constantly get taken out of the *now* and pushed into the *then* by our chatter—the thoughts in our head that pull us into the past, and the worries and anxieties that push us into the future. Your Inner Sage doesn't need to leave this moment, your mind does. Your mind is very good at going over (and over, and over, and over) what has already happened. It is also very good at worrying you about everything that could possibly go wrong in all of your tomorrows. Your mind isn't very good at being here *now* because in the *now*, it isn't needed as much. In the *now*, there is no past to rehash and there is no future to worry about. The past existed and the future will exist. But they don't exist *now*.

Of course, if you, right now, need your mind to complete a task, and it is the best tool for the job, then by all means, use your mind! Use its amazing thinking capability to your advantage. But certainly, in many, and perhaps most, of the moments in your day, your mind isn't doing anything *now*. It is instead recalling the past or concerned about the future. Similarly, while understanding your past can almost always be beneficial to you, and strategic planning for the future typically results in better outcomes, do those when they are needed, but don't let your mind stay in the past or dwell on the future when those are *not* needed. Be here in this *now*.

WHY NOW?

If it's the past and the future that keeps us out of the present, what can we do about that? And why would we want to do anything about it?

We go through our days with our minds jumping to things that have happened or fearing and consumed with things that may or may not happen. That takes our awareness out of this moment. It takes away our ability to be fully present in this moment. But when you are able to concentrate on this moment, you can bring all your energy, all your power, into the situation that you're in and you won't be so distracted by the unneeded noise.

Remember that the unhelpful noise is your chatter. More chatter moves you closer to or into the red zone, where you have very little room for even the innocuous annoyances of everyday life because you are already maxed out. Being fully present in the *now* lowers the unhelpful chatter of *then* and moves you closer to or into the green zone, where you will have much more room for the inevitable ups and downs of life. As a result, your days will belong more to you and not to the whims of worry and stress, fear and regret.

What can we do about the noise? What can we do about the past, and what can we do about the future?

You've already started doing it. You are only a few

chapters into this book and you've already begun addressing some of the thoughts and old beliefs about yourself. You've started looking at those things, and they can begin to dissolve simply by shining light on them and questioning them. Because even when those thoughts and old beliefs are hidden in the background because we don't talk about them or address them, they still influence our decision-making processes. They still affect the way we think and behave, and we usually don't even know this is happening. But by being here and reading this book, you've begun dissolving the unhelpful thoughts that drag you into the past and the anxieties that drag you into the future. This enables you to get to a place where you can more often, more reliably, be here *now*—to be in *this* moment, right where you want to be.

What else have we learned so far on our journey? We've talked about Mind Control, where you began to learn how to better be in charge of your thoughts by observing how your mind tends to race all over the place. That is a great life skill to take with you everywhere and use anytime. We've talked about learning to reconnect with and trust your intuition and wisdom—your Inner Sage. Your Inner Sage only exists in the *now*, and *now* is the only moment when you can hear it, feel it, sense it. It's like those aha moments in the shower.

Those happen because your mind was most likely taking a rare break from its past rehashing and its future machinations. In that minute, in that present-moment calm of *now*, your Inner Sage spoke up and, voilà! You had that brilliant idea, answer, or inspiration. Imagine the possibilities if you are able to tap into more *nows*.

Later in the book, we'll look at seven root causes for a lot of the noise in your head. You'll see that most of it doesn't come from *now*. We'll explore the sources of your chatter that drag you into the past, thrust you into the future, and push you into the red zone. This isn't magic. There's no woo-woo weird stuff going on here. These are simple concepts that perhaps haven't been shared with you until now or that maybe you haven't thought through before. In the end, you'll get to make decisions for yourself as to how much of your chatter you want to hang on to. You may want to hang on to some of it; it's up to you, but it'll be your choice at that point and not just something unconsciously happening in the back of your mind that impacts what's going on in your life without you being aware of it.

YOUR PAST AND YOUR FUTURE

Before we get to an Experience that will help you to be more present in the *now*, let's talk about your past and your future. Even though *right now* is the only real time that's happening—right this second, right this instant—obviously you have a past, and you will have a future, and they cannot simply be cast aside or ignored.

If you ask yourself, "How am I doing in this moment?" chances are pretty good that you're doing okay. If you ask yourself this question again tomorrow at any given time in the day, "How am I doing in this moment?" you're probably also doing okay in that moment. It's our chatter that projects all the drama, all the horror, all the pain, all the suffering, and all the worry. And then we think that every moment is miserable. Well, not every moment is miserable. *Some* moments might be miserable, but not *every one*. It's the chatter that can cloud it over and make us think that tomorrow's going to be terrible, or last week was pure suffering. Well, *perhaps* that is actually true. But in *this* moment, *right now*, you're usually doing okay.

You won't discard your past or condition yourself to be totally unconcerned about the future. But there are some things you're going to do so you aren't *consumed* by your past or your future, so you don't spend unreasonable amounts of time and energy (unreasonable, as defined by you) spinning around outside of the present.

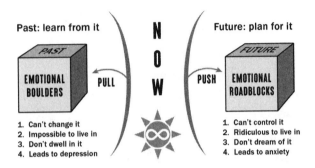

Past: learn from it

Future: plan for it

N O W

PULL

PUSH

PAST

EMOTIONAL BOULDERS

1. Can't change it
2. Impossible to live in
3. Don't dwell in it
4. Leads to depression

FUTURE

EMOTIONAL ROADBLOCKS

1. Can't control it
2. Ridiculous to live in
3. Don't dream of it
4. Leads to anxiety

Now Energy

From your past, you're going to take the lessons. You always want to tap back into your experiences, pick out what you've learned, and bring that into this moment to help you make a decision. And then for the future, you need to plan for it. You want to make sure, as best as you can, that you don't end up tomorrow in worse shape than today, and that you are moving forward toward your goals in life. But you don't want to dwell excessively in either your past or the future.

You can't always just be in *this* moment, and then *this* moment, *all the time*. But you can be aware of presence, understand it, and then experience more and more present-moment experiences in your life. These may be obvious, but they are cold, hard truths worth repeating:

1. You can't change the past and you can't control the future.

2. It's impossible to live in the past because you can only ever live in the *now*. Similarly, it's a ridiculous notion to be stuck in endless imaginary ideas of the future because you can't possibly live in the future.

3. You don't want to dwell in the past because you're then stuck in woulda-coulda-shoulda mode. You don't want to get stuck dreaming of different possible outcomes in the future since this mindset is likely full of worry and anxiety in the *now* and sets you up for frustrated expectations.

4. Depression and anxiety are likely outcomes if you're stuck in the pull of too much past or pushed into too much future.

That's the best use of the past: to learn from it without dwelling in it. And for the future, plan for it without getting stuck there. But we can't sit in this moment being afraid of them, or worried about them, or remorseful about them, or bitter or angry—that's where the misery comes from. That's the heavy baggage we're going to let go of. We don't need to drag it around any longer.

Experience: Present Moment Meditation

The Experience for Enjoy the View is a simple guided meditation. If you've never meditated, or if you're relatively new to it, you may ask, "Why meditate?" It's a fair question, with a simple answer. While physical exercises train your body, meditation is an exercise to train your mind. We are going to use meditation to bring your mind more fully into *now* and away from *then*. You'll use some simple techniques to help you quiet the noise in your head by becoming more aware of what is happening in the present moment.

This guided meditation is in three parts, about five minutes each. The first involves body awareness, the second focuses on intense listening, and the third your thoughts.

1. Body Awareness

This is a great exercise to bring yourself into the present moment. Anytime you feel your mind has you trapped in a place and time where you don't want to be, try this meditation to bring yourself into your body. You don't have to do the whole body, as even part of this meditation can help.

Sit somewhere comfortable, where you won't be disturbed for a while. Take a few minutes to settle in. Relax. Close your eyes. Give yourself the gift of these few moments. Now take a full, deep breath, inhaling through your nose and exhaling slowly through your mouth. Do that a few more times, focusing on your breath. Really pay attention to it. Feel it coming in, how it feels filling your lungs. Notice how it feels leaving your body. As you breathe in and out, see how small of a detail about your breathing you can detect.

Continue sitting comfortably with your eyes closed. There is no right or wrong way to do this. If your mind wanders, as it usually wants to do because that's what it's good at, that's okay. Bring it back to where you are, where you are sitting, and how you are breathing.

If you can, set a timer for five minutes. You are going to focus on different parts of your body, beginning with your feet and moving up until you reach your head.

- **Start by feeling your feet**. Feel the bottom of your feet. If you can do so comfortably, gently tense up some muscles in your feet and really concentrate on each foot. Feel your feet in this moment, in your shoes or wherever your feet are. Feel any sensations, or if they are hot or cold. Take several breaths while you do this.

- **Now, relax your feet and feel your calves**. Tense up some muscles there if you can, then relax them. Like you did with your feet, notice every detail you can about how your lower legs feel to you. Take several breaths while you do this.

- **Relax your lower legs and concentrate on your knees and your upper leg**. Feel what's going on there. Bring your attention, your awareness, your focus to that area of your body. Tense up your muscles there if you want. Feel what's going on right now in your upper legs and your knees. Breathe. Now relax your muscles.

- **Next, focus on your buttocks and hips**. Feel how you are sitting. How does your butt feel on your seat? Tense up your hips and your butt if you can. Do your hips feel tight? Release the tension.

- **Move on to your stomach and lower back**. Feel how your spine is aligned and how your back is positioned. Go ahead and tense up some muscles there if you like. Is your back tense or in pain? Feel how your stomach is moving as you breathe.

- **Now, move to your upper back and chest area**. Feel your lungs and your breathing inside them. If you can, tighten some muscles in your back by pulling your shoulders back. Release them and really notice how that feels as they relax.

- **Shift your attention to the ends of your arms**. Feel your hands and your forearms. If you want to make a little fist, or flex your fingers, do that. Feel what they're resting on. Feel any tactile sensation. Notice the temperature.

- **Focus now on your upper arms**. Feel into your elbows, your biceps and triceps. Flex and relax them if you can, and don't just do it casually; do it with intention, with purpose, and notice every sensation as you do so. If you have a shirt on or if your arms are resting on a surface, see if you can feel that sense of touch in this moment.

- **Turn your attention to your shoulders**. Many people hold a lot of tension in their shoulders and upper back. See if you can feel any. If you feel tension there, rotate your shoulders and then relax them. Let your shoulders droop. Breathe and relax.

- **Finally, move to your neck and jaw and face**. Move your neck side to side slightly and feel each tiny movement. Move it up and down. On your face, move each part that you can: eyes, eyebrows, nose, mouth, jaw. You move these parts of your body unconsciously all day long. Do it consciously this time. Take a moment now, keeping your eyes closed, to release any remaining tension in your body.

2. Intense Listening

Let's move to the second part, intense listening. This is another way to train your mind to pay attention to this moment. Go ahead and reset your timer for another five minutes if you'd like. You're going to listen intently and make this a game to see how many different sounds you can hear. You don't need to react to the sounds, simply listen. Notice if they are in the room with you or across the street, whether they are nearby or far away. You'll likely notice the loudest ones first. See how many more you can pick out. If you find your mind wandering away to a to-do list or somewhere else, bring it back to the listening. Concentrate on all the sounds you can detect for five minutes.

When the five minutes are up, keep your eyes closed and reflect on what you just did. You now know that if you want to focus on the moment, you have some power to do that. Your mind doesn't always need to be running; you don't need to be thinking and thinking and thinking all the time. You now have some tools to practice with, to bring your presence into *this* moment.

3. Observing Your Thoughts

Reset your timer for the last five minutes of meditation. Close your eyes again. Observe your mind and watch the thoughts that arise. You can use the mousehole tool you tried in the Mind Control chapter, or, as best you can, allow your Inner Sage to observe your mind and watch the thoughts that come up. If your thoughts start running away, just watch how they run away. Let them go for a little bit and then gently catch yourself and say, "Oh, there go my thoughts again. They're running off to a to-do list. Or they're running off to the supermarket, or they're running off to the past or to the future." Allow your Inner Sage to become the observer of your mind.

When you are finished, or when the five minutes is up, take three slow, deep breaths at your own pace. Wiggle your toes and fingers, and slowly open your eyes.

Congratulations! You just used meditation to bring you more fully into the *now*. To be aware of what is happening, right here, right now, in *this* moment. You just quieted your mind and allowed your Inner Sage to resurface and to share with you what is going on inside yourself *now*, without as much *then*.

CHAPTER 7

TRAVEL LIGHT
– Drop Emotional Boulders from Your Past –

Keep the memories.
Drop the heavy emotions.
—Tommy Stoffel

W E ALL HAVE GOOD DAYS AND BAD DAYS. We have some ups and downs, some highs and lows. That's life. We *might* have been taught how to handle the wins . . . be humble, be grateful, share it with others. We are much less likely to have ever been taught how to handle our losses— specifically, how to handle the emotions that come with the bad times in life. We're generally not taught how to *fully* experience the emotion of a painful situation, and then let it go.

What we tend to do instead is drag that emotion and pain around with us for days, years, and sometimes the rest of our lives. We stick it in our backpack with the other emotions from other situations, and now it's just a heavier load to haul around. And then another painful situation happens, and we don't know how to let that one go either, so we take it upon ourselves or we think it's our fault, and we add it to our already weighted backpack. It doesn't take long to collect a backpack full of heavy memories and emotions that feel like boulders—*Emotional Boulders*. We drag all this stuff through life with us and it can be a very heavy load.

Emotional Boulders are heavy memories from your past with an emotional attachment to them. Your past is not just your memories of events, but your memories of what happened (or what didn't happen) tied up with your emotions about those memories. That combination is what constitutes an Emotional Boulder. They're bound together. They have weight to them. In this chapter you will examine your own Emotional Boulders to decide for yourself which ones you want to carry and which ones you can set down.

Your Emotional Boulders are responsible for a good portion of the chatter in your head—the type of noise that drags you down, that prevents you from thinking nice thoughts about yourself. Emotional Boulders can lead to things like false beliefs about yourself, or at the very least, thoughts that were implanted in you a long time ago that you haven't fully analyzed with your Inner Sage. These types of thoughts can easily become Emotional Boulders that solidify the walls and bars of your cage and only serve to box you in further.

Something important to understand is that your thoughts, what you think about on a regular basis, lead to your actions. Whatever you think about leads to what you're going to do. It all begins with your thoughts. Of course, you aren't alone in the world and there are outside influences that affect you, but you need to understand that your thoughts lead to your actions, and your actions lead to your outcomes. If your thoughts are so bogged down with the background noise of stuff that happened in your past, then your Emotional Boulders are affecting your actions, which are then affecting your results, and most likely this is happening without you consciously realizing it.

Let's say you have an opportunity to move to a new city. What might happen is that almost immediately your mind will recall all the times you went someplace new and what happened when you did. If there was any fear involved with those experiences your mind is going to tell you, "Don't go. Don't go. Because last time, and the time before that . . . Remember? And remember when you were little and what happened when you went to that new place?" It drags out all the emotions, all the fears, all those boulders from your backpack, and slams them into this moment and skews your decision. This time, it may be a perfectly fun thing to do; it may be perfectly safe; it may be the best thing for you to do right now, but you can easily be dragged backward by your Emotional Boulders.

Are there a few Emotional Boulders you'd like to remove from your backpack? There's no law that says you have to carry around that old weight. There's nothing written in the ancient texts or the greatest divine books of all time or even modern psychology books that says you need to continue to suffer. You have complete freedom to free yourself from the weight of your Emotional Boulders.

LOOKING FOR TROUBLE

When you lighten the load of Emotional Boulders your thinking becomes clearer, and your true self—your Inner Sage—becomes stronger. You'll still have the memories. But you won't have the weight that continues to tie you down and unconsciously impact your life.

To find your Emotional Boulders, you're going to look inside yourself for what disturbs you. If something from your past haunts you or brings back a flood of heavy emotion when you think of it, chances are it's an Emotional Boulder. It might be a memory that is with you every day, or it might be one that only arises occasionally.

As you go looking for trouble, understand something: These things that have happened in your past can't hurt you right now. Wherever you are sitting right now, you are in *this* moment, not *that* moment, and those are very different moments. Memories of your past, and the emotions tied to them, can't become a physical reality in this moment and hurt you. They're just that—memories. This fact doesn't trivialize whatever *actually* happened. That might have been very real indeed, but now it is a memory, bundled with the emotions. It's not your current reality; it's an Emotional Boulder of a past reality. There's a difference.

If your anxiety level just went up by reading that you are going to intentionally look for trouble, that's okay. Your mind did that. Your mind has likely been trying its best to rationalize or suppress or pretend those painful memories never happened, or that they don't trouble you today. It's a defense mechanism. It's the mind's way of trying to protect you from feeling the pain from the past again. But this only masks over it temporarily until it arises again, and arise again it will.

That ends now.

Because here's what's going to happen if you don't drop some Emotional Boulders. You know firsthand that life keeps throwing challenges at you. For example, life might keep putting the same type of person in front of you that is bad for you. Until you understand *why* that type of person is bad for you and *why* you're not a match for them, then you're going to get pulled into that relationship again. If not a relationship challenge, life might throw financial challenges or employment challenges at you. It's going to keep throwing challenges at you until you learn how to deal with them in *this* moment, from what you know *now*, from your wisdom and from your presence *now*, instead of reacting from your Emotional Boulders.

Until you learn how to deal with the situation, you're going to keep getting stuck in the same old mud. And it can be painful and frustrating, over and over and over again. "This thing again? That pain again? This struggle again?" Life's going to keep giving you the same trouble until you learn how to deal with it. And when you do, and you get through it, that's when you get to marvel. That's when you will see a new horizon and know you've made it through the mud and are no longer dragging around so many Emotional Boulders.

The Experience for this chapter is going to help get you through the mud. This may sound messy, but we encourage you to trust the process. When looking for trouble, start with the small boulders. Don't go after the most painful memory you have right away. Start with something that has been weighing on you and build up to the bigger boulders. Know that it's okay to seek support if you feel a memory is too overwhelming to handle on your own.

As you go through this Experience, remember, you're safe in this moment. Keep coming back to this moment whenever you need to ground yourself.

Experience: Dropping Your Emotional Boulders

Writing down your thoughts helps to organize them, similar to how organizing your room helps declutter not just the room, but your mind as well. You feel better as a result. Writing down your Emotional Boulders will help you observe them with a new perspective and to see them as they truly are.

You now know that your Emotional Boulders are both the memories *and* the heavy emotions around those memories. So, when you write about your Emotional Boulders, write about *both* your memory of what happened *and* your emotions about that memory. Writing them down like this can help untangle the knot and separate the two. It can allow you to keep the memories and choose which of the heavy emotions you are ready to leave behind and which ones you want to continue carrying around with you.

Make a list of the things that have hurt you, the people that have hurt you, and situations that have caused you pain. Write down your memory of the situation and how it makes you feel. Be strong as you do this. It's time to uproot your old hurts and get them out of you.

One or two ideas may have already popped into your head. Start with those. Don't worry about the next one yet. Write down the first two you're already thinking of. Then write another. You're off to a great start of lightening your load. Don't hold back, get them out. Get as many of them out as you can handle.

After you've written your Emotional Boulders, review them one by one. Even though you are intimately connected to them, be as objective as possible, as if seeing them from the perspective of an unbiased third party reading them for the first time. You might also view them as your Inner Sage would, because that part of you intuitively knows what is best for you. Use this perspective to see the memories as one thing and the heavy emotions associated with the memories as another. From this decoupled perspective of your Emotional Boulders, choose which ones you want to keep in your backpack, and which heavy emotions of other boulders you want to truly let go.

Here's how people who join us on Offroad Monks journeys let go of the heavy emotions in their Emotional Boulders. Throughout the day of overcoming obstacles in their vehicle, they collect small objects and symbolically embody in each object the guilt, pain, sorrow, and shame from one of their Emotional Boulders. The objects vary but are typically stones, sticks, and pinecones. The actual object doesn't matter—it's what they represent that is important. By the time we reach the top of the mountain, people have gathered together in one place the full emotional weight of their boulders. We never ask what anyone's particular objects represent, but many choose to share. Some people choose to take a few Emotional Boulders back with them— they are not ready to let go of those just yet. Usually, several people choose a quiet spot under a large redwood tree and bury their Emotional Boulders. Some people burn them at the campfire that night. Many people choose to throw their Emotional Boulders over a cliff. All of these methods involve saying goodbye to troubles they have been carrying around for a long time. It can be very emotional and there are usually many tears shed and hugs shared. Afterward, we can see how much lighter everyone is, in their voice, in their step, and in their mood, as we almost float back down the mountain.

Consciously choosing to let go and then performing a real and tangible act of physically letting go is a very healing process. However you choose to let go of the weight in your Emotional Boulders, know that we are with you on your journey. We are confident you will feel better, lighter, and much, much freer as you go.

CHAPTER 8

CLEAR THE WAY
– Remove Emotional Roadblocks from Your Path –

Expectation is the mother of all frustration.
—*Antonio Banderas*

I
N THE PREVIOUS CHAPTER, we talked about Emotional Boulders from your past. Guess what we are going to address now? We are going to look at your future and what's blocking you from realizing the life you truly want. These blocks can come in the form of things you are dreading and are afraid of, or things you are worried and anxious about. These often-hidden fears, worries, and anxieties are future expectations, or the fear of future expectations not working out the way your chatter plans or wants them to.

Whatever your things are, one fact is certain: they haven't happened yet. Many of us are afraid and worried about what *may* happen. Sometimes you can get so afraid you get stuck and don't do *anything*. Maybe there's a roadblock preventing you from moving ahead and you anticipate things not going well, so you procrastinate.

Emotional Roadblocks are future expectations with heavy emotions attached to them. Some of the most powerful blocks, the ones that generate much of the chatter in our minds, are future-based anxiety and fear. This comes in the form of expectations of what the future will or won't bring. It's okay to have hopes, goals, visions, and to aspire to things—just don't have rigid expectations about them turning out a certain way, or when they will occur. Expectations, when sprinkled with fear and anxiety, can make for a disconcerting or even frightening future where problems are imagined and created, bringing about trouble without a cause, and putting roadblocks in your path. Emotional Roadblocks can limit your thinking, and therefore your actions. And when you limit your actions, you can restrict your outcomes. They can even drive us in the opposite direction of where we truly hope to go.

EXPECTATIONS: YOUR OWN AND OTHERS

Let's first distinguish between *your* expectations and those you may have unconsciously adopted from others. As you go through life, you pick up the expectation to be something or to have something. And yes, some of those are truly yours, but some of what you expect may come from what other people and society told you about who you need to become or what they want you to be. Parents are a prime example of imparting their expectations into their children. The media is also notorious for this. Societal portrayals of things like success and beauty are everywhere, and can influence us heavily.

There's no shortage of imposed beliefs for how you're supposed to behave, what you're supposed to look like, how you're supposed to be educated, what kind of job you're supposed to have, how successful you should be, or when and with whom you should enter into a relationship.

The media, institutions like schools and churches, government, and society in general all inundate us with a constant barrage of images telling us who we should be, but those are *their* images. And they're usually trying to sell us something or dictate our behavior. These can become adopted expectations.

Now, of course not all parental or societal expectations

are bad, or something you yourself do not also want. The point is, to overcome Emotional Roadblocks around the future, you will need to examine your expectations to gain a full understanding of their source, to see if they are truly yours and in alignment with your Inner Sage, or if they are ones you unknowingly picked up along the way and no longer want.

If adopted expectations are accompanied with heavy emotions like guilt, obligation, and bitterness, they can easily become Emotional Roadblocks in your path toward the life you truly want. They can also fuel the fires of fear and anxiety with added pressure to live up to those expectations and to be and do things that aren't necessarily what *you* truly want. Without you knowing it, they may be limiting your decisions and your own hopes and dreams for the future. Do not take on someone else's fantasy until you've fully determined it aligns with who you want to be, what you want your life to be like, and your Inner Sage signs off on it.

INSPIRED IDEAS INSTEAD
OF ADOPTED EXPECTATIONS

If you are living under the weight of too many adopted expectations, they are weighing you down, not inspiring you. If you are drudgingly going in your current direction, you aren't heading toward a good future. What you need to do instead is to flip that around and look for what inspires you to move toward the future. What do *you* want your future to look like? What kind of life do *you* want to live?

As you begin to tame your chatter and allow your Inner Sage to be heard, you'll get a clearer idea where you truly want to go. You'll be better able to clear the way of Emotional Roadblocks in your mind. You won't necessarily get specifics—your Inner Sage may not give you exact instructions with an address of where you should live and a date of when you should move and the name of a person you should get into a relationship with, but your proper guidance system will be back in place. And with that will come your inspiration. Without so much chatter based on adopted expectations, you'll dream about something you truly want to do, somewhere you've been longing to go, or something you feel driven to create. That's your inspiration. Those are *your* future visions for your life. Now you have something to aim at. And then you can establish some goals toward exactly that. You can put a plan in place to move toward the goals that inspire *you*. Then you take action and make adjustments and corrections along the way, remembering to check in with your Inner Sage so you don't wander too far off your desired path.

What's guiding you? What's pulling you forward? What's that big "Yes!" out there? Or maybe you have several. You don't just have to have one. That's a much better way to build your future than following adopted expectations and being stopped by Emotional Roadblocks. At the end of the chapter, you're going to explore what you envision for your future.

SPHERE OF CONTROL

Having expectations of ourselves is one thing, and letting go of the expectations people have put on us is another, but what can also block us from moving in the direction we want is our expectations of others. We tend to have expectations about how other people and the world should behave. But if you are being honest with yourself, you know you have little to no control over all those other things and people. In the same way that adopted expectations can mold us into someone we are not, the tightly held expectations we put on other people in our lives can limit our relationships and keep us from forming deeper connections.

You can get caught up in expecting something to happen or not to happen, or expecting someone to behave or not behave in a particular situation in a particular way. When we accept what is within our control and what isn't, we clear some debris from our path. We free ourselves from the unnecessary chatter about people and situations we have no power over, and no business trying to control.

Those expectations of others are outside of your *sphere of control* and most, if not all, of them are outside your *sphere of influence*. Your sphere of control is what you have direct control over in your life—it ends at your fingertips. Your sphere of influence, where *maybe* you can nudge things in a different direction, extends a little further, to people and situations around you, perhaps wider if you are well known.

When it comes to expectations of yourself and expectations of others—which one do you have the most say in? Obviously, it's the first one, expectations of yourself. How many of your expectations are outside yourself? Those are the ones you need to leave behind. Those are the expectations that can box you in and hold you back from focusing on the expectations you *do* have some control over.

Experience: The Expectations You Want Guiding You

This Experience is about getting down to which expectations you want guiding your life and determining what is within your sphere of control and influence. When you have these two pieces, you can move confidently into your future knowing you have power to shape a desired outcome and a vision that is aligned with your Inner Sage. You are going to write about your expectations in three parts and then you are going to score your responses to clearly show you which ones matter most *to you*.

1. Globally

Write down some expectations you have for the world. Globally, what would you like to see happen on the planet? What would that future look like?

2. Life Around You

Write about expectations you have for life around you. These are things like your family, friends, neighborhood, and work.

3. Yourself

Write about expectations you have for yourself. Write as many as you want and don't filter yourself—they don't need to sound good to anyone else.

Scoring

Once you have your three lists, review each item one by one and assign a priority to each. Remember, *you* get to define what is a high, medium, and low priority. If your mind tries to remind you what others think or expect, tell your mind, "Thank you, but please shut up. I'm listening to my Inner Sage on this one."

- Place a 5 next to the item if it is a high priority, a 3 if it is a medium priority, and a 1 if it is a low priority.

- Next to your number for priority, place a 5 if you feel the item is in your *sphere of control*, a 3 if you feel it is in your *sphere of influence*, or a 1 if it is outside both.

- Now, simply multiply the two numbers you assigned for priority and sphere to get a score for each item.

The items with a result of 9 or higher are the things you should consider doing something about because they are a higher priority for you and are within your sphere of control or sphere of influence. Those are the things for which you should put a plan in place and feel inspired that you are working toward something that is important to you and that you can and will do something about. You can work on more than one item at a time, of course, but the higher the number, the more important it is to you *and* the higher the likelihood will be of obtaining your desired results, so you might want to start with those.

Any item with a result lower than 9 is one you could drop for now. You can come back to these later, if indeed, when later arrives, these still have the same result.

We encourage you to do this Experience periodically. By choosing the expectations that matter most, you'll always have a clear picture forward, for you, as determined by you.

PART III
—
BRAVING YOUR INNER WILDERNESS

CHAPTER 9

PURE ENERGY
– Journey Deeper into Your Nature –

Energy is the currency of the universe.
You get what you give. —*Oprah Winfrey*

W E ARE NOW GOING TO TAKE YOU deeper into aspects of yourself and your life you may not have explored in great depth before. Imagine, after driving a stretch of challenging trail, you've reached a clearing. You are quite a distance from pavement and the stressors of everyday life, and you can start to see your own reflection and true nature. It's quiet and calm and you can feel your energy changing. You are determined and ready to go farther into the wilderness despite the unknowns. You have strengths and you'll use them. You have things to deal with and you will. You've made this commitment to yourself and you'll keep it.

This chapter is about energy. It is not an academic treatise full of scientific formulas and you do not need to be a physicist to get through it. There is no math. You simply need to know science has shown that if you break down any object—you, this book, truly *any* object in the universe—into its molecules, and then further into the atoms that make up the molecules, and further still into the protons, neutrons, and electrons that make up the atoms, you end up with energy.

At the minutest breakdown of what we think is hard matter, we find energy. Everything we are and everything we see is some form of energy, full of constantly moving particles and atoms. If you are listening to an audio version of this book, you are hearing it because of energy. If you are reading a printed version of it, you are able to see it because of energy. Those are different types of energy—sound energy versus light energy—but they're energy, nonetheless. You are surrounded by energy.

Most of us have had the experience of picking up on someone else's energy. Whether it's happened in a meeting at work or at home with your partner or even in public with a total stranger, you've probably experienced the situation where you just *felt something* coming from the other person. Even if you didn't know exactly what they were feeling, you sensed their attitude or things like sadness or their openness to engage in conversation. As a child, you likely sensed the energy of your parents, like the mood they were in or if there was love or anger between them. You didn't try to sense energy in these situations, you just did. You "picked up on their vibe." *Vibe*, of course, being short for vibration or vibrational energy, the unseen force that makes up the energetic quality of a person, situation, or action. You didn't feel this with one of your five senses, but you absolutely sensed it, and it was palpable.

Logically then, since you are able to sense other people's energy, they are able to sense yours. You radiate energy. Are you aware of the energy you give off and what others sense from you? Is your vibe what you want it to be?

In this chapter, you will start to see yourself as a system that emits and absorbs energy. You don't have to understand the science of it all, just understand that everything you do and everything you experience is connected energetically. The energy you emit has impact and anything you think, say, or do then has an effect on something else, like people, pets, or plants. Likewise, anything somebody else does may have an impact on you. Energy plays a part in how you see situations, in the way you see relationships and your interactions with others, and the way you see yourself. Beginning with this chapter, you are going to start looking at life from a different angle, that of the energy being exchanged.

Your energy is impacted by *your own* thoughts and emotions as well as the thoughts and emotions of others. All that energy can either lift you up or drag you down. You've felt the rush of powerful energy when everything is going your way. It feels pretty good, doesn't it? No doubt, you also are familiar with the crushing weight of energy when you feel stuck in a rut and energetically blocked.

In some ancient cultures, the energy systems in our bodies are referred to as *chakras*, a Sanskrit word that translates to English as *wheel*. There are said to be seven main chakras—or energy points—that, when open, can lift up your mind, body, and spirit. To open up these energy centers, you must learn to clear the blockages in your life. There is also some science to this wisdom. According to a 2019 research paper published by the Technical University of Munich, "recent scientific studies . . . [have uncovered that] several regulatory chakras in the human body are deeply related to human psychology. Scientists observed several regulatory micro-networks in the human body, deeply connected with immunity, health, mental peace, emotions, and happiness."[4]

Like chakras, the following illustration depicts seven major *Power Centers*, helpful energies that open up inside us, and their *Limiting Boxes*, the energies blocking us from fully experiencing our Power Centers. Whether you are more familiar with Western psychology or Eastern traditions, the energy pairings depicted here are informed by both, as well as over thirty years of personal experience and working with others to help them quiet the chatter in their minds. Regardless of your familiarity level with the source of these energy pairings or your beliefs, most of us can appreciate the positive energy shown in the Power Centers and see the value in moving away from the negative energy depicted in the Limiting Boxes.

First off, what are *Power Centers*, and what are these *Limiting Boxes*? Power Centers are things you *are*, your natural state of being, such as safe, confident, authentic, and free. The Limiting Boxes are things you can *have*, internal energy blocks that prevent you from freely accessing your own

4 N.J. Cooper, "A Brief History of the Chakras in Human Body," University of Munich (technical report), March 2019, https://www.researchgate.net/publication/342562977_A_Brief_History_of_the_Chakras_in_Human_Body.

personal Power Centers, such as worries, fears, and despair. These negative energies are the chatter in your mind that inhibits, agitates, and confuses the natural energy of your Power Centers. This chatter is the hard cement that is holding all the bricks in the walls of your Limiting Boxes together. Throughout the next seven chapters you will learn about each energy pairing in more depth, and how to free yourself from what is blocking you and move into your grab-life-by-the-steering-wheel power.

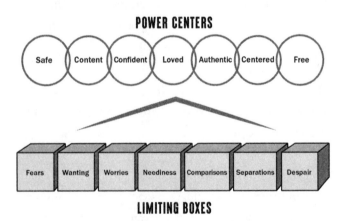

Power Centers and Limiting Boxes

It's good to keep in mind that these energy pairings, like much of life that isn't so black and white, do not exist in isolation from each other. They are connected and there is overlap because they support and inform each other. For example, there is an element of fear in all seven of the Limiting Boxes, and your Limiting Box of worries may have some fear of embarrassment or fear of failure in it. Similarly, when you begin to feel more safe, you'll naturally begin to feel more confident, and with confidence comes a greater ability to share love. Because of this connected energy flow, any work you do in each chapter can reduce the size of each subsequent Limiting Box, and therefore you will likely find the chapters feel lighter and more doable as you go.

Collectively, all seven energy pairings make up the vibe you give off—what others will pick up from you. If your Power Centers are mostly open, people will sense that intuitively. If you are stuck in your Limiting Boxes, people will also intuitively know this about you.

Your Limiting Boxes are built from the yellow and red zone chatter in your head. If not reined in, this chatter will deplete you. Chances are, if you're struggling at work, can't hold a healthy relationship, are feeling bored, lost, anxious, or angry, one or more of these Limiting Boxes has a hold on you.

You were not born with Limiting Boxes and their negative energy. You were not born with fears, wants, worries, neediness, or despair. You were not born constantly comparing yourself to others or feeling separated from the people and the world around you. You picked these things up along the way. That is great news because if you picked them up, you can set them down.

You set them down by reducing the chatter that built the boxes that are blocking you from moving toward your Power Centers. One of the simplest things you can do to move toward anything in life is to remove what is in your way. By reducing the chatter that is strengthening the Limiting Boxes, you will naturally move toward your Power Centers. Simple, right? But not necessarily easy, so beginning with the next chapter we are going to focus on breaking apart one box at a time so you can, step by step, begin to open up each natural Power Center.

You can approach this like a treasure hunt to find what is blocking you. Each of us will find different chatter that built our Limiting Boxes, and we can't tell you what you will discover. That would be like us telling you what an apple tastes like when the only real way to know is for you to taste the apple yourself. Have fun finding things out about yourself, and be excited about what you may find within.

You may not have the same level of positive or negative energy in all seven pairings. You might be more toward the Power Center of one and closer to the Limiting Box of another. As you continue your journey through the remaining chapters, you may find the level of chatter blocking you in a particular area is relatively low, and therefore that Limiting Box is much easier to break apart. Other Limiting Boxes of yours might be stuffed full of raging red zone chatter. Those chapters might be more important for you. If you have a particularly troublesome box, set it aside and come back to it later. You'll find that as you break some of your boxes apart, even just a little, you get stronger, and opening them further becomes more doable. And then, cracking open even your most impenetrable box will absolutely be possible for you.

Experience: Assess Your Energy

Look at each Power Center and Limiting Box. Based solely on how each one makes you feel, rate yourself as green, yellow, or red.

Green means you are good to great with that one. Yellow means it's not your strong suit, but it's also not dragging you down terribly. Red means it's a thorny issue for you. Don't overanalyze this. Go with your gut feelings and write down your self-assessment. Yes, your rating will probably fluctuate over time or depending on circumstances, but *overall* in your current life, how do you feel about each one?

Power Centers	**Limiting Boxes**
1. Safe	1. Fear
2. Content	2. Wanting
3. Confident	3. Worry
4. Loving and Loved	4. Neediness
5. Authentic	5. Comparison
6. Centered	6. Separation
7. Free	7. Despair

As you reflect on what you wrote down next to each energy, you may instinctively start to notice a pattern. For example, if you are in the red zone with fear, you might be somewhere in the red or yellow zone with safe. If you gave content a green, you may notice you gave wanting a yellow or green as well. At a quick glance, you can begin to see how the energies are interconnected. This Experience is simply to let you know your beginning baseline level for each Power Center and Limiting Box before moving on to the remaining chapters, where you will go deeper into each energy pairing.

CHAPTER 10

REDUCE YOUR FEARS AND BE SAFE
– You Can Only Scare a Frightened Mind –

Fears are nothing more than a state of mind.
—*Napoleon Hill*

IN THE HIERARCHY OF HUMAN EXPERIENCES, being safe is a fundamental requirement. We all naturally need physical safety, like food, clothing, and shelter. We all need things that promote personal safety, like good health and financial resources. In this chapter, we'll explore beyond those physical needs to look at emotional safety—and the lack thereof.

As we head a bit deeper into your inner wilderness, you'll explore the root causes of what makes you feel emotionally unsafe. If you're not prone to self-reflection, this may very well be the most unexplored terrain of your journey. It may have even been off-limits until now.

The primary negative energy that blocks us from feeling safe—your natural Power Center—is fear.

Fear can be complex, both in its origins and how it manifests in your life. Fear can be your biggest roadblock to becoming the best version of yourself because it is ancient, primal, and powerful. Fear is rooted in one of the deepest and oldest parts of your brain—the amygdala. This is your fight-or-flight center, and it is estimated to have begun evolving around 200 million years ago. That's a heck of a head start over your awakened and aware self that is reading this book now.

Fear comes in so many forms, shapes, and sizes. There's fear of change, fear of failure, fear of disappointing others, fear of *being* disappointed. Fear of rejection, fear of abandonment, fear of making a mistake, fear of success. Financial fears, job fears, relationship fears, fear of the unknown. Fear of illness, and ultimately, fear of death. There's no shortage of fears and they can pile up fast. This chapter will help you understand your fears better, both the ones you admit to and those you won't.

Fear may present itself openly in your life and with your full awareness. For example, if you are afraid of speaking in public, you may avoid it at all costs. Fear can also be unknown to your conscious mind and stealthily rob you of potentially beautiful life experiences. For instance, if you didn't feel loved and accepted as a child, or if you had failed romantic relationships earlier in life, you may have unconscious fears of rejection, abandonment, and not being good enough, so you don't approach people as often or as openly or as your authentic self as you might if you felt safe in sharing those emotions.

The problem with fear is that it grips us tightly and keeps many of us frozen in place, afraid to try new things. It causes a lot of red and yellow zone chatter in our heads, and a lot of anxiety, pain, and suffering. More often than not, the fear-fueled chatter is your mind trying to keep you safe—safe from the unknown or safe from being hurt again—and it runs around and around in your head without you ever questioning it. This can keep us stuck, physically and emotionally. But being overly afraid is not the way to feel safe. Examining your fears closely and then letting some of them go is what will help you feel truly safe, which you will get a chance to do for yourself later in this chapter.

IMAGINED FEAR VERSUS REAL DANGER

An important thing to know about fear is that there's a distinction between real fear and imagined fear. Real fear is when you are in danger. Actual danger. Not imagined danger. Real fear is when you're driving down the road at night and all of a sudden, the headlights coming at you swerve into your lane. That's danger. You are going to react instinctively and immediately—by stepping on the brakes and swerving out of the way. That's real fear in an actually dangerous situation.

In this chapter, we want to talk about the imagined fear—the fear we create ourselves, and the fear that's created for us.

There's a common saying about what this kind of fear is: *False Evidence Appearing Real.* Fears we create ourselves are numerous. If you have kids, you may know the fear and anxiety we can create when our child is sick, and we spin a cold into something much worse in our minds. Or you may take an innocent comment by your boss and turn that into the fear of losing your job. All of that imagined fear is red zone chatter in your mind.

A big fear we can create for ourselves, especially as men, is what we call *fearlings*—the fear of your feelings. Many men stuff their feelings down. *Way* down. It can feel safer to focus on the transactional necessities of day-to-day life than to deal with your feelings. It's not uncommon for men to feel more competent dealing with things like the never-ending pursuit of "success" than facing their feelings. Societal expectations can also make men think they need to always be stoic and impervious to pain. If you have fearlings, now is the time to deal with the fear. If you don't handle your feelings, they will handle you.

If you watch any of the high-drama news shows and get caught up in all the fear and anxiety they present, that's a perfect example of fear being created for us. It can create lots of head noise and chatter and will absolutely move you toward, or into, the red zone. Chances are extremely high that the situations they are scaring you with are not a factor in your everyday life, or are at least not as bad as they are making them out to be. It's highly unlikely those fear-filled situations will have much impact on you today, tomorrow, or for the foreseeable future. But of course, fear sells.

It's not that your fears aren't real to you, because fear can absolutely feel very real in our minds. Everyone has some fears and they're as real to one person as they are to the next. But you need to draw a distinction between what's in your head and what's really happening in your life to distinguish real danger from imagined fear.

Try this experiment: Stop paying attention to the news for a week. Any and all news. World news, local news, celebrity gossip. Ignore it all, even the headlines. For a full week. Then, check in with yourself at the end of the week. If you feel even a little less fearful and anxious, you have some simple proof that the news isn't helping you. Just like you are what you eat, your mind is what you feed it. Garbage in, garbage out. You can then make a choice from a place of knowing as to how much energy you want to absorb from the news.

A lot of fear comes from the thought or feeling of losing something or somebody. We're afraid of losing our wealth or our health. We're afraid of losing whatever it is that we've collected—be it friends, relationships, or our toys. Another common fear is being afraid of something happening, or not happening, in the future. Usually, it's something that *might* happen, or *might not* happen. Try to catch yourself when your mind is on these fears. You can then do an objective assessment as to whether this is a real danger and you need to deal with it, or if this is your mind imagining unlikely possibilities. If it's your mind creating chatter around imagined fear, it's only strengthening your Limiting Box.

Whatever the sources of fear in your mind, you need to ask yourself a few very important questions about fear itself. What *is* fear? What, *precisely*, is fear? *And where* is the fear? Fear is thoughts. It's neurons firing in your brain. Broken down to its root, that's what fear is. You may ask, "Why does fear have so much control over me? Why does it cause so much hardship in my life? It's just thoughts in my head."

Again, we are not suggesting you ignore real danger and problems in your life. On the contrary, we have suggested making plans to address those, and to do so from a place of less chatter and more alignment with your Inner Sage. But it's good to discover that at least some of the fear that causes you so much hardship in life is likely between your ears. Why is that *good*? Because now you are gaining some control over what goes on between your ears! You can take control of your own thinker once you know what it is and what's going on in there. It's not something "out there" that you need to fix or wait for someone else to fix for you. Your fears are thoughts in *your* mind, that *you* can manage and change your perspective on. That's great news!

Let's take the simple analogy of walking into a pitch dark and unfamiliar forest. You may be afraid of bumping into rocks or tripping over tree roots. You simply don't know what is in front of you. You don't know what's in the woods that can hurt you. But then you turn on your flashlight.

Now you can see. Now you can assess what you need to avoid, or what not to bump your leg on. By shining a light on your fears, literally or figuratively, you gain awareness, and your fears can then be more fully understood. This can make some of your fears disappear and others much more manageable. When the light goes on, the darkness fades. This chapter is your flashlight.

Maybe you've been afraid of sharks ever since you saw the movie *Jaws*. Is that a real or imagined fear? Did you know that you are six times more likely to be killed by a pig than a shark? Pigs are indeed more dangerous than sharks, so are you now going to be afraid of pigs? What about ants? Ants are also deadlier than sharks. The point here isn't to minimize or make light of any of your fears. The point is to look at your fears rationally and objectively and decide for yourself if you want this fear to limit your life or box you in. As Tommy says, "You can only scare a frightened mind."

The truth is, most of what you're afraid of will never happen. So decide whether you want to hang onto those fears or not—it's your choice. You're an intelligent human being. You get to decide what to do with your fears. Are they serving you? Maybe you have some concerns that *are* serving you, protecting you, or protecting your family. If so, work with them. But if they're blocking you from doing something, if they're holding you still, or if your feet are cemented to the ground because of particular fears or anxieties, then you decide if you want to bust that box apart or stay stuck in it.

Consider this possibility: You wake up one day at a late stage in your life and you realize that because of fear you didn't do things, behave in certain ways, interact with people the way you meant to, or accomplish things the way you wanted to. You didn't allow your inner light to shine brightly. You lived small. You've got a large pile of remorse in your past and now you're going to close your eyes for the last time and this is the way you go out. Don't let that happen to you. Wake up today.

YOUR SAFE POWER CENTER

Your Safe Power Center is founded on a solid bedrock of truths about yourself and your life that do not rely on others' stories or beliefs about you. It's knowing your strengths, your weaknesses, and your values through a deep and honest assessment of yourself.

Emotional safety is being able to accept both praise and criticism without identifying with either. It means not letting the praise inflate your ego or the criticism deflate your heart. Instead, you know that praise and success can inform you about what works in a given situation, and that criticism can spark some self-reflection to determine whether that feedback also rings true with your Inner Sage. If it does, you can determine whether that is an area in which you'd like to make some changes and improvement.

Emotional safety is knowing you are whole and complete as you are, no matter what life throws at you. To sense this, visualize yourself as a circle representing how you came into the world—whole and complete. As you travel through life, you enjoy some successes and discover good things about yourself, and you also pick up some bumps and bruises along the way. After a while, your whole and complete self looks less like a circle and more like a piece of a jigsaw puzzle, with some bumps sticking out here and some dents over there. *But you are still whole and complete.* Of course, there are things you want to change and improve, in yourself and your life—that's why you're on this journey—but you know that no matter what happens along the way, you aren't broken.

Yet our fears can make us doubt that. Prior hurts can fill our minds with imagined fears of them repeating, and this steals away from our natural feeling of being safe, whole, and complete, the way we came into this world. Fear can make us doubt ourselves and our abilities so much so that we live and breathe by the praise and criticism of others instead of standing strong in knowing our own intrinsic and undeniable value, imperfect as it may be.

This is why part of this journey is to find daily or regular activities to center you in safety. One simple thing you can do is get into nature. We all know it's good for us and we don't require further proof because we all feel better after a day of hiking, fishing, off-roading, or being at the beach. It helps calm many emotions, like stress, anxiety, worry, and fear, and you feel more emotionally safe as a result. It is so very easy, however, to get stuck in cubicle-world and meeting-mania, bumper-to-bumper traffic, job-site snafus, and working long extra shifts. Before you know it, days and weeks have gone by and the only places you've spent any significant time are inside buildings and vehicles and *that* is not natural.

Getting outdoors doesn't have to be complicated. Your *mind* will want to make it complicated by rattling off an endless list of why this is a stupid idea and how you don't have time and it's not on the to-do list and on and on. Tell it to shut up and get outdoors anyway. Your Inner Sage knows this is good for you and that you haven't come this far on your journey to sit in your vehicle the whole time.

To stop your mind from overcomplicating something

humans have been doing for eons, don't bring the inside out. Meaning, don't bring all your head noise with you when you get outdoors. BE outdoors. Be fully present in your surroundings. Pay attention to everything around you. Notice not only the really big and obvious, like the sky and mountains, but look closer and try to notice the small things, like how the breeze feels on your skin, the differences in the songs of the birds, or how many shades of green you can see.

Being fully present in nature will ground you. Center you. Remind you that you are energetically a part of this earth you call home. You are made of the same vibrating molecules and atoms as everything you see around you. You are home. You belong here. This is a profound sense of security.

We have a special Offroad Monks shortcut for you. While you are outdoors, go barefoot. As Clint Ober talks about in his book *Earthing*, when you contact the earth with your bare feet or body, commonly called *earthing* or *grounding*, electrons from the earth's surface flow over and into you, which research has shown to have numerous natural benefits, including reduced inflammation and stress, while improving sleep and mood. Reconnect with Mother Earth and the *now*, and you will return to a place of safety within you.

Experience: Facing Your Fears

This Experience will help you look at your fears in a new way and decide for yourself which ones are real dangers and which are imagined, as well as which ones you want to hold on to and which ones you are ready, willing, and able to let go. You'll be able to bring your fears out of the dark recesses of your mind and into the open.

Maybe your fear is admitting you even have fears. You wouldn't be the first guy who didn't want to admit to *anyone* that he is afraid of *anything*. As guys, we tend to deny and hide fear and pretend we aren't afraid because we think it's seen as being weak. There might be times where that is called for, but that is usually when we're in front of other people. Right now it's just you, so now is the time to be completely honest with yourself. Nobody is looking over your shoulder to see what you write down. Don't cheat yourself by lying about your fears here.

By reducing the constraints of the Limiting Box of fear, you will naturally move back toward your more natural state of feeling safe inside yourself. If you don't do this Experience to diminish the negative energy trapped in your Limiting Box of fear, it will still be there, feeding off every recurrence in life that resembles the source of that fear, growing stronger and louder each time. You'll still have the same old fears, in the same old places, and even if you manage to stuff them down again, your fears will find their way back to the surface.

Facing your fears head-on may be challenging, but you've denied or suppressed them long enough. It's time now to deal with them and strengthen yourself as a result. Think of each fear as a weed. You don't want to just get rid of part of the weed or it will grow right back. You need to dig down and get at the root and rip the entire thing out. As part of this Experience, you'll try as best you can to trace backward and find the root of your fear. If that proves to be challenging, do it anyway. It's worth it.

Go ahead and write down your fears. Pick the top three to get started. Add more if you have them, whether they are big or small. Do not limit yourself. You don't need to share this with anyone, ever, so don't hold back and don't judge. You don't have to get rid of all of them, or all at once, so go ahead, be brave, and list some things you are afraid of.

When you've finished, go down your list one by one and dig deeper into each fear by asking yourself these questions:

- Where did this fear come from? What is my first memory of it?

- Is this fear a real danger to me or those close to me? How so?

- Is this a fear I want to keep? Why? Can I address it?

- Is this a fear I want to let go of? *Can* I let it go? *Will* I let it go?

- Can I do anything about the thing I fear? If so, am I willing to do it?

- Is this fear within my sphere of control? My sphere of influence? Or outside of both?

- Am I ready to dig this fear out by its roots and drop it?

Remember that even though you might dig out a fear by its roots, that doesn't mean it won't come up again in your life when a similar situation occurs. You may recognize the fear as being similar to one you decided to drop. This simple awareness and understanding can diffuse a fear that previously would have stopped you in your tracks.

Any fears you can lessen will allow you to naturally feel more safe.

CHAPTER 11

REDUCE WANTING AND BE CONTENT
– Leave This Mud Pit Behind –

If your desires be endless, your cares and fears will be so too. —*Thomas Fuller*

THE SECOND ENERGY PAIRING we are going to deal with is the Power Center of being content, and the Limiting Box of wanting. While positive energy clearly exists in contentment, we want to be clear that there's nothing wrong with wanting things. Indeed, wanting can be a great motivator to move forward in life toward the goals and relationships you envision for yourself. But unending and ever-changing wants and desires for more, more, more can't be sated. They will only strengthen the Limiting Box that prevents you from being content.

Often, what may drive this insatiable wanting is when the desires you are pursuing are not actually your own but ones you unknowingly inherited or adopted from those around you or society in general. If a desire is rooted in others' expectations of you, when you finally do get what you believed you wanted, you may be left feeling empty and unfulfilled, which keeps you chasing more. You can end up spending your life trying desperately to achieve other people's idea of contentment instead of your own. It's time to look closely at your wants as your newly reawakened Inner Sage to make an honest assessment of where they came from, whether they are yours, and whether they bring meaning, purpose, and contentment into your life.

If you have found a sense of discontentment about yourself or your life, be it consciously known or a vague undercurrent that is subtly troubling you, this chapter will help you uncover why you are always looking for more or wanting what you don't have.

One of the reasons we can find ourselves consistently chasing *more* is because we are chasing a bottomless well of happiness, rather than the stable and easy flowing stream of contentment. First, let's distinguish between being happy and being content. Happiness, like sadness, tends to come and go, and usually that ebb and flow is due to outside sources, like other people and situations. You'll likely be happy if you get a raise at work or your favorite team wins a big game, but after a while that happiness will fade. Similarly, you may feel sad for a while if you get turned down for a date or passed over for a promotion. Being content is more consistent and comes from inside you. You can be content with your current level of income and if you get a raise—great! You can be content with who you are inside and the qualities you bring to the table even when you get a no on that date or promotion. Happiness is a state of mind. Contentment is a state of being.

Being content doesn't mean giving up or giving in. It's okay to want things, and to want things to change. But, by your own judgment, if your wants and desires have become too many or too onerous, or worse, have turned too much toward greed, you simply won't be content. That's a miserable way to go through life.

Excessive wants and desires can keep you focused on the future, thereby putting off the peace of being content. Contentment tends to keep you in the *now* and allows you to be more fully present with what is. Unending wanting can keep your attention on what you *don't* have, whereas being content keeps your attention on what you *do* have.

MATERIAL WANTING

The most common connotation of wants and desires is, of course, that which involves material things—mainly money and possessions. When it comes to your wanting tangible trinkets, only you should decide how much is enough. If you live in an unsafe house in a dangerous neighborhood, or drive a car that breaks down often, it certainly doesn't feel like an unhealthy desire to want a nicer place to live or a more reliable means of transportation. If, however, you want a bigger, better, fancier place to live and a brand-new car in order to keep up with a friend, a neighbor, or some image presented by the media, that's when you need to question whether your Inner Sage is in charge or not. Especially if such a desire poses a financial hardship. Keeping up with the Joneses is a surefire way to keep yourself down.

You should ask yourself, on a regular basis, where the wanting for material items comes from and if it is truly in alignment with who you have chosen to be. Ask yourself if this is a want or a need. Be prudent and responsible about whether you can afford it, and objectively assess the impact acquiring it will have on yourself and those around you, especially anyone who relies on you financially.

Everything you acquire has a weight. It must be cared for, maintained, watched after, protected, upgraded, replaced.

If your to-do list or your time is dominated by tasks related to taking care of your stuff, perhaps it's time to ask if your possessions are possessing you. Or perhaps you're fairly successful financially and you have help to take care of your things—housecleaners, a handyman, a lawn mowing service, a pool service, regular pest control, a CPA to prepare your taxes, a nanny to help with the kids, and an assistant to run errands for you. Be sure your servants haven't become your masters. Are they helping you or does it feel like you are working for them? Ask yourself this question periodically because those things can get away from you an inch at a time, and by the time you realize it you may be miles from who you want to be.

Material wealth, or the lack thereof, is relative. There will always be people with more or less than you. This isn't a race or a contest. When you are reviewing your life in your final days, you won't be reflecting on your possessions or whether you ended up with more or less than other people. Unless you know their financial situation intimately, all you really know about the people who appear to have more toys than you is that they *spend* money, not that they *have* money.

Being content with enough, as defined by you, or with less than you have now, will remove a boulder from your shoulders. You won't feel the constant weight of the nagging need to always be striving for more, more, more. You can finally catch a break and relax a little. You'll be freer financially, which can free up some of your time, money, and energy to do more of what truly brings you peace or to be more generous with others. You'll be more content with what you *do* have without needing to expend resources to get more of what you *don't* have. A little minimalism can go a long way toward maximizing your contentment. It's okay to get rid of objects and desires that no longer serve you. It's okay to downsize to the right size. As Tommy says, "When I got to a place where I didn't want anything, I got everything I needed."

Ask yourself the following questions to determine if your material wanting is in alignment with who you have chosen to be:

- What are some material things that I want?

- Do I really want those things, or am I doing or getting them for someone else or for an unconscious reason?

- Do I really need that new car now or is it because a coworker showed up in a shiny new one and everyone seemed impressed? Is this to fulfill instant gratification or would it be better to drive my old car for another

year and commit to adding that monthly car payment
to my savings every month?

- Am I acquiring something because of the fear of missing
  out? Or because I'm trying to make up for not having
  enough in my past, perhaps in childhood?

- Am I being sucked into the mass consumerism of
  society because of advertising or peer pressure?

- Will this material item give me something I value in
  life? Will it bring me joy or brighten up my days? Does
  it educate, inspire, or bring ease to my life? Would it
  make me feel more content?

There are no right or wrong answers to these types of life
questions. After all, it's your life. Just make sure you are living *your* life and not someone else's. If you don't figure out
what you want in life, life will do that for you. If you don't
live *your* life, you'll live a jumbled mishmash of everyone
else's. Add and remove things from your life for the right
reasons—*your* reasons.

INTANGIBLE WANTING

We humans are such diverse creatures that there is no real
end to our intangible wants and desires. Attention, love,
power, and acceptance are common desires, as are job titles,

praise, recognition, and control (usually of others). Your desires might even be more supernatural or ethereal, like awakening or enlightenment. Most of them are personal and subjective.

To help you find your own, as you continue to pay more attention to the chatter in your mind, notice how much of it revolves around you wanting or longing for something nonphysical, perhaps related to the wants we just mentioned or something intangible that you *don't* want. Thinking about wanting less of something is the other side of the same coin of wanting something. Maybe you want less responsibility, self-judgment, worry, shame, fear, pressure, or expectations.

A tricky thing about your intangible desires compared to your desires for physical items, is that the reason you have them is more likely to be unknown to your conscious mind. You may have been justifying this desire for so long (or even outright lying to yourself about why you want it) that your conscious mind simply accepts the reason as truth. Due to the mental gymnastics our minds are capable of, it can be a little trickier to find the root source of an intangible desire, which can make it hard to decide whether it's really yours or it came from someone else. It's one thing to discover that your desire for a new car every two years goes back to being embarrassed as a child when your father drove you around in his old rusty clunker. It's a whole other depth of realization to learn that all the years and money you spent getting a certain degree has its roots in your years of striving and striving to gain your father's approval or get him to like you. Or that you married young and repeatedly because you were desperately trying to feel loved by a woman because you grew up with an emotionally absent mother.

Sometimes we can end up justifying our intangible desires simply because they are unseen and we think they are not as big of a deal as buying that new house with an ocean view or acquiring other material things. In doing so, we often underestimate how the unseen could be running our lives and driving our decisions. Just like with your desires for physical widgets, be sure to check in with yourself on your desires for intangible things, too. Whether it's your next vacation, or that promotion and its fancy job title, or a life partner with certain specifications, or even any type of serious relationship at this point in your life. Your desires for things like respect, recognition, or love can be just as powerful, and you need to challenge them just as closely.

Similar to how you questioned your wanting of physical objects, be curious about where your desires for intangibles are coming from and whether they align with who you choose to be now.

Ask yourself:

- What are some of my intangible desires?
- Is it the right time to add this to my life?
- How would I feel emotionally if I added this to my life?
- Do I really want this, or am I doing or getting it to make someone else happy or because I feel like I'm supposed to?
- Am I doing this for a reason I can't explain?
- Am I doing this to impress someone?
- Am I doing this to get people to like or accept me?
- Do I want this because someone else or society expects me to want it?
- Would gaining the object of my intangible desire make me a better person? Would it improve my life in ways that are important to me? Would it improve the lives of those around me? Would it make me content?

We encourage you to keep an eye on what you want. Watch your chatter for clues and see what comes up, then try to determine where it is coming from. In a minute, you'll have the opportunity to do a root cause analysis to help guide you toward finding the source of your desires.

The good news continues to be that this Limiting Box of wanting, like the others, is between your ears. It's full of conditioning and chatter you've picked up along the way, usually unknowingly, and now that you are much more aware, you get to decide what to keep and what to jettison. Remember, what's in your head is the stuff most in your sphere of control. In a moment, you're going to have the option to drop some of your wants, or at the very least to edit them down drastically if they're no longer serving you and you've instead become a slave to them.

When we can let go of misaligned wants, when we can parse out what desires are truly our own and not inherited or implanted by our surroundings, we can more easily move toward our Power Center of being content.

Experience I: Evaluate Your Wanting

This Experience is a technique you can use now and in the future to weigh what you think are important desires and make sure they are in alignment with who you choose to be now.

Our goal here isn't to make a value judgment on your desires. Instead, we want *you* to make a value judgment, objectively and honestly. And you can't do that if you don't know where they come from or why you have them. Only with full awareness and understanding of the what, where, and why can you then have the informed experience of consciously keeping or purposefully changing or dropping a desire.

Write down your top three desires. You can eventually do this exercise for all of them, but it's okay to begin with just a few. They can be tangible or intangible, in any area of your life, including relationships, your financial situation, a job or career, or education. As always, don't overthink this or pass judgment. Simply make a list and leave additional room to write under each item.

For each desire on your list, write down your responses to these questions:

1. How long have you had this desire? What is your earliest memory of it? When was the seed planted?

2. What is the source of this desire? What inspired it? Where did it come from? Did it come from inside yourself or outside yourself? Did it come from another person like a relative, friend, or teacher? Did it come from an institution like church, government, or the media?

3. Imagine you have this desire met today. How would you feel? Go with your gut; tap into your Inner Sage, and be honest about how you'd feel. Does it feel positive or negative? Is there fear or anxiety, or do you feel joy? Thumbs up or thumbs down or somewhere in the middle?

This Experience brings awareness and understanding to your wants and desires, and from this place of knowing you can now choose which to keep, change, or drop. This Experience may validate your desires as truly something you want to spend your time and effort pursuing. Great! Use that as further motivation to move toward those. You may find parts of a desire work for you, but some of it does not. That is also great news because now you can keep what works and drop what doesn't to better craft the desire into one more in alignment with your Inner Sage. And if you find some wants and desires you no longer wish to carry around in life, that's even better news! You can now have the experience of self-realization and freeing yourself from those. Make the decision to drop them and then cement that decision with a physical action like having a ceremony to burn or bury the desires you've written down. Or tie each one to a rock and throw them off a cliff. Writing them down, getting them out of your head, and then getting rid of them helps remove all the chatter surrounding them in your head.

Experience II: Material Contentment

This is optional, but if you are up for an additional challenge to get your material desires under your control, then here is an extra Experience for you to have. Track your expenses for a month. All of them. Don't be selective and only track some of them because you already know what's hiding in them. Don't conveniently forget to include those couple extra drinks you paid for with cash when you were out with friends. As we've said before, you are only hurting yourself if you lie to yourself.

At the end of the month, sit down as your Inner Sage and see if where your money went aligns with who you want to be. If you have a spouse or partner with comingled finances, you should do this together. Look at each category of spending and ask yourself if, by your own judgment, you received a satisfactory value for the amount you spent. You might find some areas where you spent more than feels right with the direction you now choose to head. You might find the opposite in some categories, that you wish you'd spent *more* in that area. This isn't about "good" spending versus "bad" spending, or spending money on virtues or vices. This Experience isn't to get you to go out with your friends less often and buy flowers for your mother more. This is about you looking at your spending and deciding for yourself if your expenses are in alignment with your values.

Do you like where you are spending your money? Are you saving enough? Is your credit card debt a burden?

Make adjustments based on your own assessment. Do this Experience for a few months, or ideally every month, until you get your spending more in tune with your chosen life. Then keep going.

CHAPTER 12

REDUCE WORRIES AND BE CONFIDENT
– Worry Will Drive Off with Your Strength –

Worry does not empty tomorrow of its sorrow.
It empties today of its strength.
—*Corrie ten Boom*

B EING CONFIDENT IS ABOUT internal strength. It's your determination, will, and courage of character. Confidence is your sense of inner knowing that you can handle whatever comes your way in life. This doesn't mean you have all the answers, all the time, in all situations. It means knowing that you, and your resurgent Inner Sage, are strong enough and resilient enough to assess things that come your way in life, make sound decisions as to the best path forward for yourself and those around you, and that you have the resolve to proceed, knowing you can make adjustments as needed as you go. It means knowing that any mistakes or falls are not failures, but lessons containing the gift of additional information and experience that further strengthens you as you stand back up and proceed again.

The Limiting Box that prevents you from being your fully confident self is built from your worries. Worry can make you think things won't turn out well, which may give you a reason to not even try. Worry can make you think you can't do something and that because you didn't succeed previously, you won't succeed this time. Like all the Limiting Boxes, worry has some fear in it. There is also some wanting in worry. Worry is a fear of things not unfolding as desired. The only thing longer than the line at the DMV is a list of possible worries, and this chapter is where you are going to explore yours.

WHAT IS WORRY?

What is worry? You may say, "Well, I worry about this, and I worry about that," and yes, we all have worries, but what, *exactly*, is worry? And where does it come from? Is worry "out there"? Outside of yourself? Is your bank account a worry? Are your bills a worry? Your job? A relationship? Everyone has worries, and while yours might be quite legitimate in terms of being life situations you need to address, your list of worries is *not* worry itself. They are things you *worry about*. Worry is not external, but something internal and within your control. To break this down further and tell you something you probably don't want to hear, your worries are things *you choose to worry about*.

That's what worry is: a choice. It's giving way to anxiety or unease and allowing your mind to dwell on difficulty or troubles. Worry is a way you choose to respond or react to a situation. It's choosing to go beyond what is necessary for strategic planning and instead thinking excessively about a situation in the false belief or hope that it will make a difference. Many people get stuck thinking that if they just worry long enough or hard enough, then the thing they are worried about will be affected and turn out the way they want.

People can get very defensive when told their worries are a choice. They will insist that they *need* to worry about this and that and the other thing, or else! Some people are worry warriors and are quite proud of their worrying. They are proud of how many things they can worry about, how much heaviness they can hold on to and drag around with them while still seemingly functioning smoothly in life. "Look how much worry I can handle!" They can become like a martyr, attached to, identified with, and proud of the amount of weight they carry around every day. Wouldn't life be lighter, easier, and more fun if you were trapped less by your worries? Wouldn't you feel more confident, stronger, and more alive?

Here's another thing about worry: We often think that when we pay off that bill, or land that job, or find that relationship, then the worry will go away. It doesn't quite work like that. Your mind is *always* going to find something for you to worry about. It's your mind doing its job of trying to protect you from anything going wrong and getting you to prepare for all possibilities. It *never* ends. Worry is an internal addiction. You likely aren't making a conscious choice to do it. You probably don't say to yourself, "I need to worry now," but you can't help it. You worry without trying.

Here is a simple example to illustrate how worry is a choice. Let's say two people are trying to get to a very important meeting on time. Perhaps it is a big presentation they have to give or an important job interview. They are standing next to each other on the curb at a busy intersection in a busy city and the meeting starts in five minutes.

They are running late, and they realize they won't make it in time. They have to now try to find a taxi. One of them gets knotted up inside and panics. They eat themselves up inside with worry and anxiety that escalates and grows with each passing minute. They tell themselves that if they don't get there on time, then this bad thing will happen, and if that happens, that will mean this other bad thing will happen, and so on. That chain of worry goes on and on until they've worried themselves into one catastrophe after another. The other person thinks, "Well, I can't control this situation very much. I'm going to do my best to summon a ride, but I can't control how fast we get across town or when I get there. I just have to accept what's going on and I'll deal with it when I get there, whenever that is." Same situation, two different choices. One is addicted to worry and, indeed, knows no other way of coping. The other understands their sphere of control and sphere of influence and decides on a plan to take action, but is not eaten up inside with worry.

Worry-Go-Round

You've probably noticed that when you worry about something you don't just worry about it once or twice and then relax. Like everyone else, you've probably been stuck in a worry loop, repeatedly worrying about something and looping back to begin worrying about it again. And again. And again.

You've also probably noticed your worry loop about one thing is usually followed by a worry loop about a different thing, which is followed by yet another worry loop about something else. Worry loop after worry loop. Pretty soon you are on a never-ending worry-go-round of worry loops, and you are now worrying about something so far removed from the original worry loop that you've worried yourself into a very agitated state.

Maybe you worry about your car being unreliable. If your car dies, then you won't be able to get to work, and you worry about losing your job. If you lose your job, then you can't make the mortgage payment, and you worry you'll have to move and take the kids out of school and away from their friends and away from their grandparents who help watch them after school, and you'll have to find new childcare with people you don't know and that will cost even more money. From a relatively small life situation to be addressed, you've managed to excessively worry yourself into anxiety about much bigger things.

Worry-go-rounds can lead you to doubt your ability to handle it all because you aren't worrying about *one* thing, you're worrying about *many* things. This self-doubt and insecurity destroys confidence.

WORRY YOUR WAY TO NEGATIVE ENERGY

The anxious state of worry can create a lot of negative self-talk. That leads to very unhelpful chatter that pushes you into, or higher into, the red zone. If you are always worrying things will turn out badly, or that people will think less of you, or that you might fail or embarrass yourself, then you are focusing more on the negative energy of worry and less on the positive energy of the very thing you want to accomplish.

In chapter 9 we discussed how everything is energy. Negative self-talk is *negative energy*. Try to catch yourself when you do this and instead, think and talk more about how you will feel when you accomplish whatever it is you are setting out to do. Tune in to the positive emotions you might feel around accomplishing a goal and let that guide your thoughts. Combine your thoughts with the energy of your positive emotions and your thoughts will become so much more powerful. Remember, your thoughts lead to your actions, which lead to your results.

Let's take the case of trying something new in life and the worry that might go with that. You should expect that if it's something new to you, whether a new job or learning to play the guitar or gaining control over your chatter, you are not likely to be very good at first. Don't apologize for this. It's normal. You're learning. Prepare yourself as best you can, of course, but give yourself a break and don't worry so much about everything that *might* not go so well, and certainly don't give up. You may not remember this but as a child you didn't give up when you fell down while learning to walk, did you? Of course not. Partly, that's because back then you had not taken on the external worry of the adults around you. You didn't know yet that you "should" be worried about falling down and getting hurt or being embarrassed. Worry will limit your confidence. When trying something new, you could use more confidence and less worrying.

Most of the things you worry about never happen, anyway. In our experience, 99 percent of the stuff you get overly worked up about never occurs. You create an untold amount of drama in your head and your life for this 99 percent of stuff that never happens, at least not to the degree you've worried about it. Yes, once in a while things do happen that you've worried endlessly about. But guess what? In that 1 percent of the time, if your mind and energy weren't stuck in the negative energy of worrying about the 99 percent of the stuff that never occurs, then you'd be more confident in dealing with it. You would be much more present in the moment and have a much clearer head to deal with it because your mind wouldn't be caught up in all the other silly noise coming from worry. By worrying less, you'll be much more confident, much more aware, and much better able to handle difficult challenges when they present themselves. When that 1 percent of stuff does happen, look for the lessons in there. Look for what you can learn from that situation and carry the lessons forward with you, not the worry. The lessons will be much more useful to you in the future than the worry ever will.

So the next time a challenge arises, instead of thinking and thinking and worrying and worrying about all the things that could go wrong, imagine all the exciting possibilities of things going the way you want them to. Genuinely positive thoughts and feelings will give you confidence and bring a positive energy to your actions. Simply by thinking positive thoughts, you can drastically increase your chances of experiencing positive results. It's all about energy, and yours is well within your sphere of control because they are *your* thoughts, in *your* head. Who has the most control over *your* thoughts? You do. You can be confident of that.

It doesn't take much to start. Even if you can only shift

your thoughts and energy away from worry just a little, and only on a few occasions, you'll still notice that you're more decisive and clearheaded. You'll build confidence. Your Inner Sage will get stronger. Your belief in your ability to figure things out will grow. You'll move away from the negative energy of worry and toward the positive energy of your inner confidence. Knowing where you *don't* want to go *and* where you *do* want to go is more powerful than either one of those by themselves.

The choice is yours, now that you know. The next time you catch yourself on a worry-go-round, you're more likely to recognize it and think, "Aha! I'm doing it again!" Then you can choose to stop spinning around and around and get off. This is probably going to take some practice because your worry habit is deeply entrenched, but it will get easier the more you practice, so give it a try. After a while you'll be able to catch yourself at the beginning so you can get off quickly.

Of course, you won't just stop all worrying all at once, but when you understand what worry is and you understand its source and function, you'll be able to begin discerning between a *concern* and a *worry*. There is an Experience at the end of this chapter to help you make the distinction between concerns, which are life situations you should address, and worries, which you can do less about. As the

Dalai Lama said, "If a problem is fixable, if a situation is such that you can do something about it, then there is no need to worry. If it's not fixable, then there is no help in worrying. There is no benefit in worrying whatsoever." You can live without worry but you'll likely always have some concerns, which are worries brought into awakened consciousness, and it's better to live with some well-understood concerns than a head full of never-ending worry. Strategize and solve your concerns as best you can given the information and skills you have available to you. That is a much better use of your energy than spinning around in worry.

Chance, Control, and Cost

There are three important Cs for you to check when you have a worry: chance, control, and cost.

Chance

What are the chances this will really happen? They are probably slim, but make an honest assessment. Also ask yourself if this is happening right now, which makes it more of an immediate concern to be addressed, or if this is somewhere in the nebulous future.

Control

What is the control factor? Can you control this situation? Does it make sense to expend your energy futilely worrying about something over which you have zero control? You know about your sphere of control and your sphere of influence, so consider this question carefully and expend or conserve your energy according to your own value system.

Cost

What is the cost of the worry? How much energy is it draining from you? Is it worth that cost? What level of stress is this causing you? Are you waking up early because of it? Not able to get to sleep? Are you less able to be the father, husband, employee, or student you want to be because you are distracted by worry? Is your physical or emotional health suffering? After worrying about this for the umpteenth time, do you feel you have solved the problem, or do you feel drained? What's this costing you, and are you okay spending that much energy on this particular worry?

Experience I: Apply the Three Cs

For this Experience, write down a complete list of all your worries. You know what they are because they are swirling around as chatter in your head every day. If you've never made an actual list, now is the time to take a different approach and get them out of their sole residence between your ears and onto paper. Writing just a few words about each is fine, but the more detailed you can be, the more worry words you'll move out of your mind, at least temporarily.

For each worry:

- Apply the three Cs described above. Assess the chances that what you're worrying about will actually happen, your control of the situation, and the cost. All three should be determined by you, with the help of your intuitive Inner Sage, of course.

- This is optional, but assigning a numerical value may help you with letting go of some worries. For each of the three Cs, assign a value of 5 if you rate it high, a 3 if you rate it medium, and 1 if you rate it low. Now multiply the three values together for each worry. Worries with a smaller score are ones you should consider letting go first.

Maybe there are some things you worry about that have a high chance of actually happening, and you have a good deal of control over the situation, and therefore you have a concern you feel you should address. For others, perhaps the cost of that worry is simply too great. Most likely you'll find at least a few things you worry about which you have little to no control over *and* which are unlikely to become a reality. Catch yourself when you get on a worry-go-round about those and get off as soon as you can. With a clearer picture of your worries, you'll be more confident in addressing some and letting others go.

Experience II: Bury Your Shit

This next Experience will help you to find the source of your deeper worries. This isn't for your lesser worries about things like the weather or traffic—you can use the first Experience for those. This is for your bigger, foundational, long-held worries. Often your worries are about future outcomes you can't predict, unknowns, and unmarked roads you've never traveled. Other times, your most troublesome and nagging worries are based on long-held fears of experiencing the same pain you felt in the past—these are the worries you will address in this Experience.

Let's say you have repeated instances in your past of people dying on you or abandoning you in one way or another. That can easily become a constant worry in the back of your mind—that the next relationship you get into is going to end because the same thing is going to happen again. You're worried you are going to be abandoned or the person is going to leave you by death or by choice. This is how past hurts, past violations, and a desire for them not to happen again can gang up on your present moment and make you worry about a similar pattern of behavior repeating itself. So yes, you might take a look or a comment by your spouse and spin that into a worry-go-round about them leaving you, but the reason you react in such a way could be traced back to past situations in your life.

Because it's happened in the past, you worry it will happen again. This can eventually result in you getting exactly what you expect. You are actually attracting that negative energy because you believe it may happen to you at any moment.

Another example: perhaps you haven't had great success at holding down a job so, when you do get one, you constantly worry about losing it. Beginning a new job with the nagging worry that you won't be able to hold it down, that you'll be no good at this, and that you'll fail for sure can bring about the same outcome yet again. This pattern of worries only undermines your confidence, keeps you from taking action, and holds you in the past.

In both cases, your chatter mind thinks that worrying about something is a solution to avoid the pending catastrophe that you believe is going to happen. It becomes a self-fulfilling prophecy. Not only is worrying not doing you any good, but it's actually making things worse.

Painful situations and hurts you've suffered in the past can be a source of your worry today. They can plant the original seeds of thoughts like self-doubt and self-incrimination. You'll begin to think you aren't good enough, that you aren't worthy. The worry you feel today from those past situations can be compounded if you experienced them as a child, when you probably took them on not knowing, not understanding, not being able to process them, not being able to fight back or argue against them. These hurts may have become part of your belief system and may be eroding your confidence, burying your courage, and weakening your will.

This Exercise is an opportunity to excavate the worries buried in the darkest corners of your mind. Explore this Experience as intensely as you can because your conscious mind may not be aware of what deep worries from the past are still impacting your thinking, decisions, and indeed, your life. Worries from these deeper places can be pretty hidden and covered up by stories you've been telling yourself to justify their existence.

You are not going to simply list your worries—you are going deeper than that. You will be writing about the people that have hurt you and situations that have caused you pain. You are going on a mental mission to release a lot of old crap that you may not know is hiding there. Go as deep as you feel ready to venture on this stretch of your journey, and remember you can always pause to look at the view or seek out support along the road.

You are going to use a technique we call *scribblish*. Scribblish is where you scribble your thoughts on paper as fast as they come to you, and it's okay to write gibberish. Your thoughts will come *much* faster than your hand can move, which is why we created scribblish. You'll be writing so fast you won't even be able to write complete words—sometimes all you'll manage is a letter or two. Nothing you write needs to be legible because it's not necessary that even you ever read this again. You can do this on a keyboard, but we prefer good old-fashioned pen and paper. The energy released by furiously scribbling as fast as you can, knowing it is messy and unreadable and full of spelling and grammatical errors—and you don't care—is liberating. So, get the perfect paper for you—maybe a full-size sketch pad or perhaps colored paper. Get the perfect writing tool—maybe a black marker or a red felt tip pen so you can imagine your thoughts staining the paper as they flow out of you.

When you are ready to get the shit out of your head . . . GO!

Write one horrible thing that happened to you, a time when someone hurt you or took advantage of you, or a situation that caused you pain. Start scribbling and don't stop until no more shit comes out. Scribble thoughts, memories, feelings, worries, emotions, names, dates, places, events, words people said, smells, tastes, song lyrics, and every possible detail that comes to mind. As fast as you can. Don't think about what you're writing. Don't edit as you're writing. Don't go back and reread as you're writing. Don't care about any logical order. Just keep scribbling in gibberish. And *do not stop* until you are empty.

When you finish, rest for a bit—you just did a lot of work!

The physical act of scribbling out your angers and frustrations and hurts and violations can be enough to get them out of your system. It's like what we have people do on the trail, when they make their biggest obstacle in life into a boulder and then drive over the damn thing. It's the same concept and it works great. The deeper you go, the more you'll clear, and the better you'll feel forever.

If you want further closure, you'll need to bury your shit. It's time to bury the heavy emotions you've detached from your memories and scribbled down on paper. It's time to bury the old and heavy worrying you've spent so much precious life energy on. Take the paper you've written on, or print it off the computer, and then bury it somewhere. Bury it deep; bury it in a place where you'll never see it again. Bury it under a tree or under a giant boulder. Bury it and cover it with cement. Just bury it and you'll be done with it. You'll have a lot less chatter instantly. It is simple and yet not too simple. It's how it works, and we've seen it work many times.

REFLECTING ON YOUR JOURNEY SO FAR

We were born in this society, we grew up in
this society. And we learn to be like everyone else,
playing nonsense all the time.
—*Miguel Ruiz*

BEFORE WE BEGIN the Power Center of loving and being loved and its corresponding Limiting Box of neediness, let's take a few minutes to review your journey so far through the untamed wilds of your inner world. Has it been rockier than you expected? Smoother? Were you worried or fearful going in? How do you feel now? Did you think you'd make it this far and go this deep? Take a minute to acknowledge your strength and courage to uncover your Inner Sage and do this important energy work. You've traveled quite a way. You have a bit further to go.

Along the way, you have been setting down some heavy Emotional Boulders from your past and letting go of some Emotional Roadblocks from your future. The work you are doing will absolutely move you forward in life, but it will also get you back to where you came from and where you most naturally belong.

You naturally came into life with your Power Centers in place. You're naturally safe. You're naturally content. You're naturally confident. You're also naturally caring and empathetic and loving. And you're naturally yourself. On this journey, you've been uncovering what's been there all along.

Rediscovering your natural way is being true to yourself, your uniqueness, your authenticity. You're naturally aware of what's going on around you, and you're naturally connected with everything and everybody that's around you. That's the way you are; that's your true nature. You naturally have a sense of wanting to be fulfilled and to enjoy what you're doing.

All the walls of all your boxes that keep you from your natural way of being were built up over many years, usually without you knowing it was even happening. You picked up your Limiting Boxes from other people in your life and from society's conforming norms, and they feel like jail and not like you because *they aren't you*. Not your natural you, anyway. Now you know that anything you picked up along the way can be dropped along the way, too.

Choosing for yourself which Limiting Boxes you no longer wish to stay stuck in and doing the work to dismantle them will free your true self immensely. Your chatter will quiet noticeably, and you will be in or closer to the green zone much more often. Your Inner Sage will emerge a bit more, a bit stronger, and you'll hear your inner wisdom a bit better.

You'll be better able to recognize and understand that when things pop up in your life, and they will, you can self-correct and say to yourself, "You know what? I'm choosing differently this time. I'm choosing to not pick up another worry. Because now I know what worry is, and I'm not going to do that anymore." Or "I'm not going to get into this thing of always wanting and desiring more, because I don't need to play that game anymore." Or "I'm no longer going to react to that person or that situation in the same way because that is negative energy and I choose to bring more positive energy into my life and the situations and people I interact with."

It's a choice. It's *your* choice. You're going to be able to choose whether or not you want to take on those boulders going forward, and to choose what you want to let go of, or what you want to hang on to. It may not have been a choice up until now because nobody taught you this. But it's your choice now.

This won't be an overnight process. You won't snap your fingers and make all the negative energy suddenly stop flowing your way. Your life won't turn overnight into nothing but sunshine and cake. You've got some work to do. You need to take responsibility for your thoughts, choices, and actions. It might be a small, perhaps barely perceptible change at first, but when you shift your thoughts, choices, and actions—*your energy*—even just a little, the change will expand; the change will grow, and soon you will "*be the change you wish to see in the world.*" Remember the analogy of turning a ship at sea. If you shift your energy even just one degree, you'll be heading in a new direction, and soon you'll be in a vastly different place energetically.

Now, on to your Power Center of loving and being loved, and its Limiting Box of neediness.

CHAPTER 13

REDUCE NEEDINESS AND BE LOVING AND LOVED
– Let 'Em Off Your Hook –

If you're helping someone
and expecting something in return,
you're doing business, not kindness.
—*Unknown*

COUNTLESS BOOKS HAVE BEEN WRITTEN about love, and deservedly so. In this chapter, we are going to focus on one area of love that tends to make relationships more challenging and less fulfilling than they need to be. And it's an area you can do something about by doing the Experience at the end of the chapter. We aren't naïve enough to say all your relationships will become perfect. But some of them could be better, and when it comes to arguably the most powerful Power Center of them all, loving and being loved, it's worth trying.

The area of love we are going to focus on is conditional and unconditional love and how the Limiting Box of neediness blocks you from being in your natural state of love.

Unconditional love is just that—love without any conditions surrounding it. It is not propped up by demands and it does not exist only if certain conditions exist. It is genuine and true, full of kindness, caring, and compassion. Unconditional love is without judgment or expectation of love in return. There is no "What's in it for me?" thinking. Unconditional love is a feeling, a sensation, an energy.

Conditional love is thought-based love. It must have conditions met to exist. It comes with judgments and expectations from the chatter-filled mind. Conditional love is only given *if*—*if* you behave a certain way or *if* a certain thing happens or *if* you love them back. It is not freely given. Conditional love is to unconditional love what a plastic rose is to a real rose—they may look and feel similar, but you know they are not really the same at all. To be truly loving, you don't need anything in return.

When we're not in touch with our Inner Sage and we still rely too heavily on our chatter brain in living life, we get conditioned to believe we must be loved by others. Love is seen as a need. A need we can't fulfill ourselves. A need we don't recognize the true source of. We are raised and conditioned to believe love must be earned. As such, we become dependent on the love of others to validate ourselves and to feel we are worthy of another's love. The truth is your life, and the way of your Inner Sage is one of pure love. Without knowing this we go on a mad hunt to feel the love our Inner Sage knows is everywhere. The chatter-filled ego-mind, thinking love must be searched out and acquired like a rare jewel and paid for with approved behavior, goes seeking it from others who may also be seeking unconditional love. But thinking we'll find love only if we meet someone who satisfies our list of criteria for love is thought-based love, not unconditional love. Until the shift is made within from a limited supply of thought-based love to the ever-available, heartfelt, unconditional, energetic love, a love seeker can feel needy, clingy, and even desperate.

Seeking love from others also seeking love can quickly become needy, where a co-dependency may develop where both parties are *thinking* about love and the need for love in all the wrong ways.

THE ORIGINS OF CONDITIONAL LOVE

We came into this world as bright, glowing, love-filled babies without any Limiting Boxes of conditions weighing us down. We loved without prerequisites or expectations.

The transition to conditional love began early. The idea that we were either a "good boy" or a "bad boy" or a "good girl" or a "bad girl" began very young. We began collecting labels quickly, such as being good at school or bad at sports or known as the quiet one or the rambunctious one or the smart one or the funny one. There is an endless supply of labels and categories, and at least to begin with, they are mostly put on us by those outside of us. Thus begins our dependence on a condition of approval from further back than we can remember. This can go on for years and decades and it accumulates inside us, building the walls of our boxes.

This conditional approval—the idea that if we do this, we'll get rewarded; if we don't do that, we'll get something taken away, or we won't get the "good boy" or "good girl" affirmation—starts to become this inner split in ourselves. "Am I good, or am I bad?" It starts training these confusions and dependencies, and it can lead to a need for approval, a need for attention. This builds our boxes over time, and we don't even know it's happening.

This is not a condemnation of parents, caregivers, teachers, or family members. They didn't necessarily do anything wrong. It's just the reality of the way it happens in the world. They are most likely simply repeating the same behaviors under which they were raised. Child raising in many societies is based on approval and disapproval ratings to manage behaviors. Children raised in cultures heavy in self-centered chatter, which is how most of us were raised, learn love wrong. Instead of being raised with loving acceptance, we're trained to believe love is conditional, and we perpetuate the cycle until we learn a different way and are able to break the cycle.

This awareness is meant so you can understand now, as an adult, where and when you might have picked up some of your sense of conditional love. It may be from very far back, before you were anywhere close to wise enough to be aware of what was happening, much less able to decide for yourself how you felt about it, and so it became a part of the foundation of who you think you are.

Over time, people can build up a need for certificates of approval. Where they once needed their parents' approval, they now need approval from a spouse, a child, a boss, or a coworker. They might unconsciously need approval from pretty much everyone to validate that they are desired and loved, good and virtuous. When approval is mistaken for love, people can easily become addicted to needing an endless stream of approval from others, a condition we call *approvalitis*. This need for approval leads to trouble because the relationship then becomes needy and clingy and one can become dependent on other people to feel good about themselves.

HOW WE PUSH BUTTONS AND SET HOOKS IN CONDITIONAL LOVE

When our love Power Center is blocked and we are disconnected from our source of unconditional love, we can find ourselves in a messy game of tug of war in our relationships. *Pushing people's buttons* or *setting hooks* in *people*—these are everyday metaphorical phrases that represent the energy in relationships that are not based on unconditional love. Hooks and buttons are a form of approvalitis, showing us where you may be trapped in the mindset of associating approval with love.

People are very good at pushing other people's buttons (*you* are probably pretty good at it too) to make them feel or act a certain way. We are best at this with the people closest to us because we know them so well. We know exactly which buttons to push, when to push them, and how hard to push them to get the reaction we seek or to elicit the behavior we desire. If the love in a relationship is based on conditions, people frequently use button pushing as a control mechanism in an attempt to get those conditions met. The reason your buttons can be pushed in the first place is because you are allowing them to exist. By caring so deeply about what others think, or by unconsciously seeking their approval, every one of your buttons is up for grabs.

The hook setting comes in when you have a relationship with somebody where you have a need for their approval. If your need of their approval means you would do anything to keep them close, and you desperately want them to love you back, you have a hook in your heart that can be used as a control mechanism. It can be used to get you to do or not do something, or to get you to behave in a certain way. It's good to have emotional connections with people, but it's the dependency on it and the fact that somebody can play that against you, or you can play that game against them, that we are bringing to light.

These buttons and hooks are part of the energy dynamics in entangled relationships. When we are stuck in cycles of approval, this means we have triggers within that make us susceptible to the relational conditions, expectations, and controls of others. With both buttons and hooks, the energy flows both ways. Frequently, we play these energy games with others unconsciously. You might have entangled dynamics with people at school, or work, or in your personal relationships. Maybe you have a boss you need to please. Maybe you have a partner that loves you when you behave in a certain way and pushes you to act that way.

Some people walk around in their lives like energy vending machines, allowing others to push their buttons all the time, making them feel crappy, making them feel sad, draining energy out of them. You don't need to be somebody's energy vending machine anymore if that's a role you play in relationships.

Pay attention to the buttons and hooks in your own relationships—and the disharmony this can create and how it can limit your Power Center of loving and being loved. Anytime someone tries to control or change someone else in a relationship, it does not make for a healthy, accepting, loving dynamic—this is the opposite of unconditional love. Maybe you have friends that haven't explored their inner world as you are doing and are like a black hole, sucking up all the energy around them. Friends like this might see your light beginning to shine through and unconsciously set a hook in you and latch on, trying not to go under themselves. It's not their fault. They know not what they do. They're simply playing the only game they know. This is where your consciousness of the dynamic becomes important. You need to be aware that this happens because then you have the ability to start letting some of these go and not letting people push and pull you around.

And if you are the one pushing other people's buttons or putting hooks into them, whether purposefully or not, ask yourself why you're doing it. What are you getting out of making someone else feel bad? Does making them feel bad make you feel better? Ask your Inner Sage if that's the kind of energy exchanges you want in your life. If you're the one setting hooks or pushing buttons, all in some misguided or unconscious attempt to make someone react, behave, or change, you are going to have the chance to stop.

A goal of a truly free relationship is to be free of buttons and hooks on both sides. Since you can't control the other side of the relationship, the best course of action is to unhook your own hooks and unplug your own buttons. In the Experience for this chapter, you'll be able to do just that. Getting to a place where you no longer need approval—a place without buttons and hooks—is possible in any relationship. This is genuine love. Full acceptance. No conditions. This degree of relational freedom may sound unreal or difficult to reach, but it is the ultimate goal of a truly unconditional, nonjudgmental, emotionally free human-to-human relationship.

Spotting the Push and Pull: Entangled Terms

Listen to some of the terms we say to each other in relationships and about love. You can feel the energy in these terms that reveal the hook and button connections between us:

- Stop pushing my buttons.

- You're stringing me along.

- Stop yanking my chain.

- I'm a puppet on a string.

- I'm hooked on you.

- Let's tie the knot.

- Let's hook up.

- We're bound to be together.

- Family ties.

- Family bonds.

- Wrapped around my finger.

- The ties that bind.

- I'm all tied up in knots.

Listen to how . . . *entangled* those sound. Listen to how limiting those sound. What if instead, you were simply loving? And let others be loving if that's what they choose to be? No prerequisites. No conditions. No buttons. No hooks.

UNCONDITIONAL, UNLIMITED LOVE

We know what unconditional love feels like because we felt it as a baby. We felt it, perhaps, with our own newborn child. Maybe you have some relationships now that are like that, where you both feel unconditional and unlimited love for each other. They are easy to be with. You love them no matter what crazy stuff they do. That's the unconditional piece. There's no neediness. There are no hooks. There's no button pushing going on. It can take some work to get there in some relationships, and it may not be fully attainable in every relationship, but we hope people can find or create at least a few relationships in life like this. It is certainly doable on your end, even if the other person in a relationship can't or won't get there.

You have within you the ability to give as much love as you want (you won't run out), and to do so without demands or conditions. We tend not to do this, to give unlimited and unconditional love. Maybe we've done it in the past and then somebody betrayed us, or they didn't love us back in the way we wanted and we felt the painful sting of rejection.

The sudden loss of love through death, betrayal, or rejection is arguably one of the worst feelings we can experience as humans. It's heartbreak and it hurts. Bad. Perhaps it comes with the death of a loved one or even your pet. Perhaps it comes with the shocking misbehavior of your partner. Perhaps you are dumped. Many of us experience this emotional tragedy, and when we do, if we don't have a loving counselor or friend to help guide us through the mourning period, there's a good chance that wound will never heal. When that happens, we swear never to get hurt like that again.

We then withhold love, reasoning that it's too painful to love anymore, afraid to give love so freely in the future to new people and situations we encounter. We close up. We shut down. We build our walls. All in the name of protecting ourselves.

Any walls you build to protect yourself will also keep out the love you want. There are no one-way walls. With the Power Center of loving and being loved, if you've built impenetrable walls to protect your heart, know those same walls limit the flow of your love outward to the people and things you want to love in your life, and they limit the possibility of love flowing into you. You may have managed to protect yourself, but by blocking so much potential love from friends and intimate others, you've also managed to hurt yourself. As you break apart those walls, you'll be freer to both give and accept love, unconditionally and in unlimited amounts.

With your walls firmly in place, your sensory capabilities of your Power Center of loving and being loved are limited, blocked, and boxed in. This diminishes your capability to feel, trust, and know your feelings, which means your mind has to take over and observe every situation you're in to think (not *know*) if you're safe and secure, in a loving situation, or in a place of trust. That mind analysis of every situation creates an extensive and exhaustive amount of additional chatter in your mind, and can quickly launch you out of the green zone into the yellow and even red zone for a good part of your life.

When you clean your relationships up using the Experience at the end of this chapter, you can dismantle your defensive walls and freely give love again. There will no longer be a need to be afraid of somebody taking love away from you or hurting your feelings because you won't be imposing conditions and you won't need their approval. They will no longer have hooks in you. They will no longer be able to push your buttons. They won't have that power over you anymore.

YOUR SIDE OF THE EQUATION

How are you going to untie all these hooks and unplug all these buttons? You probably saw this answer coming, but it's up to you to let other people off the hook and it's up to you to stop reacting to their button pushing. You aren't going to go around telling others to stop pushing your buttons and to take their hooks out of you. You can't just go out and say, "I read this book and you're going to not hook me anymore and you're not going to push my buttons anymore."

You don't need to confront the other person. That's not likely to work anyway since, as you know, they are outside your sphere of control. Instead, you are going to take on the responsibility to detach from your end. You are still going to have relationships, but they're going to become much cleaner and clearer, richer and fuller, deeper and more meaningful, and they're not going to have that potential to pull you down or drain your energy. In his book *The Four Agreements*, Don Miguel Ruiz said, "I will no longer allow anyone to manipulate my mind and control my life in the name of love."

Some people may be pushing your buttons and yanking your hooks on purpose, knowing you'll react, *wanting* you to react. For those people, it's even more important to do the work of disconnecting, and quite honestly, to possibly let that relationship go entirely. They may still throw hooks at you, hoping to sink them anew and deeper, or they may push your buttons more frequently and harder. But you'll be in a place where you understand their energy game and, instead of reacting, you'll decide for yourself how to respond, or to not respond at all. They may still thrash around and flail away and behave in their usual manner, but you can choose to simply not accept their hooks and to unplug the buttons they are pushing so they no longer work. You are now in a place where you understand, from a new place of compassion and empathy, the greed and the fear and the worry and all the sources of people's Limiting Boxes and that *those* are why they do most of the things they do.

You'll see a friend or a family member or somebody at work coming toward you who has always had the ability to make you feel bad, or to irritate you, or to drain you, or to put you down. Now, however, you can choose to think, "Okay. Bring it on. I'm not giving you the reaction you want." At first, they're going to pull their stunt, and you may step out of the way, or you may just let it pass through you, or maybe it will hit you and bounce off. But you'll be *responding* instead of *reacting*, and those are very different. You'll be responding from your Inner Sage and from your new place of awareness as to the root causes of their behavior.

It may take a few times for you to get better at responding in the manner of your choosing, and for them to realize you are no longer playing their energy game. Be strong. Eventually, you'll get to a place where, if you want to be in this relationship, you'll be able to catch their arrow and give them back a rose. You'll be able to turn that relationship into something different and give them back something that will dissolve the undesired hook and unplug the unwanted button and replace them with a much more open, loving, caring relationship.

Experience: Untangle Your Relationships

The Experience for this chapter is in four parts and will begin the process of teaching you how to untangle some of your relationships by unhooking hooks and unplugging buttons. This is not a one-and-done experience. It will need to become an ongoing practice for you.

Part I: List the Impactful Relationships in Your Life

List the names of all the people who have the ability to change your mood the most. People that can make you happy. People that can make you sad. People that change your energy in any way, for better or for worse. Maybe it's parents, maybe it's kids. Spouses, partners, family members, friends, coworkers. Living or deceased. People currently in your life or people from the past whose memory affects you. Everyone is fair game. You know your relationships, especially the ones that trouble you. Now is the time to change them. If you don't unhook on your end from the relationships that aren't working, you're going to continue getting yanked around. If you want that, it's always your choice. If you no longer want to be pushed and pulled, that is also your choice. Write your list without limitations and without judgment. Open up and let it flow through and out of you. Feel the energy of each of those relationships as you write their names or initials.

Part II: Prioritize Your Relationships

Next to each name, write a 1, 2, or 3. Relationships with a 1 are the really tight relationships, the really close ones, your inner circle. Maybe that's only two or three people in your life—a partner, a parent, a child—that you have really tight bonds with. Those with a 2 are your next circle of family and relationships and friends. Number 3s are everybody else on your list. Your outer circle. Maybe a work relationship, like a manager or a boss or a subordinate, or perhaps a neighbor.

Part III: Imagine Untangling

Do this visualization practice first on your number 3 relationships. You'll want to work up to your number 1 relationships. You want to do this on a tier 3 relationship to get some practice because, beginning now, you're going to interact a little differently going forward. Choose a tier 3 person, someone that has the ability to negatively change your mood, irk you, or piss you off. Someone who has the power to make you feel a way you don't want to feel.

Do an imagination exercise. Close your eyes. Investigate that relationship by looking closely at it and understanding how they make you feel and in what situations they trigger your emotions. In your mind's eye, see the hooks that are set there, feel the buttons they push. Feel that tug, from an emotional standpoint, of how they get to you. Go deep inside with this one. Fully bring up the feelings of that relationship. Bring up a real situation that happened, and feel that discomfort, the way you felt when you interacted with that person and they played one of their games. Feel it like it's a hook in your heart or a button just waiting to be pushed.

Now, imagine going in, reaching into yourself with your hand, and *unhooking that hook* or *unplugging that button so it no longer works*. It may hurt. It may feel like you're letting something go that's been there for a long time, something that feels like a part of who you are, and that it's finally time to let it go. You might hesitate. Feel that struggle. It might be a lot or a little, but *unhook that hook and unplug that button on your side*.

Let yourself off the hook. You play a part in this relationship, too. So, forgive yourself and release any guilt you feel. Chances are if they're pushing your buttons, you're probably pushing theirs. Let that go. Forgive yourself. Let go of any guilt, or shame, or anything else you have in that relationship. And of course, let them off the hook and forgive them. There's no finger-pointing; there's no blame here. People can do some pretty horrible things to each other, and some pretty horrible things can happen to us. This isn't about being okay with those things or situations or people. It's about releasing the hold they still have on you. See if you can find forgiveness in your heart. Forgiveness can be helpful in detaching the hold these events and people still have on you. Find forgiveness for your own sake. You're not forgiving them so they get a pass. You're forgiving them to set yourself free.

Part IV: Respond Instead of Reacting

For the fourth and final part of this Experience, take this one step further and imagine the next time you interact with this person. Go to that place where you're going to see this person again. Imagine that encounter. Feel how the relationship is already different because you've removed the hook and unplugged the button. You know what they're going to do. You know the hook is going to be yanked or the button is going to be pushed.

Now, imagine how you're going to respond differently this time. Not react. Respond. Reacting is when you fire back. They push your button or pull that hook and you get angry and yell or whatever your reaction normally is. But that's what used to happen in this relationship. Now you have clarity about what's going on, and now you're going to choose how you respond. Your response may be that you simply don't fire back. Or that you're silent. Or that you say, "You know what? I don't want to get into this anymore with you. I'm not going to play this game anymore." Whatever comes to you now because you have this awareness, will be with you when you face that situation for real in the future. With practice, it will get better. You'll be able to shift that relationship on your end out of this energy draining place so that you can either find a healthier, unconditional way of being with that person, or you can end the relationship altogether.

Once you do this with a tier 3 relationship, you'll feel how much better that relationship has the potential to be. Less painful, less stressful. More positive, more freeing. Then, you're going to do this to more relationships and clean them up. Practice with a few tier 3s. Then move on to some of your tier 2 relationships. Practice. Get better, get stronger. And then you'll be ready, willing, and able to do this on your tier 1 relationships. You are taking back your energy. Nobody has the right to take it away from you (and you don't have the right to take others' energy). We just give away energy because we don't know what we're doing. Now you do.

Here's an important part of this process: *you're not going to tell people what you're doing*. You're not going to say, "Hey, I'm unhooking my hook with you." That person is probably going to be surprised when you don't react like they are expecting. Not consciously surprised, perhaps, but unconsciously they might think, "You know what? Something didn't work here. I usually walk up to this person and I act a certain way and I get a response out of them. They get huffy, or they get angry, or they get upset. I get some energy out of that." It's not good energy; it's playing below the line, but they're getting energy. When you don't give them that energy, they're going to sense that something isn't right. They may try a different technique to jab you somewhere else, or to yank on the hook a little harder, or to push a button in a different place. Watch for that. Watch how people act and react, and just be aware that they may step up their game a little bit. They're probably not doing it consciously so don't get angry at them. That's just the dynamics of the game they're playing.

Fishing is a good analogy. Somebody's fishing for your energy. If somebody is fishing and the fish stop biting after a while, at first they may take their stinky worm and add some power bait to it. They may dress it up a little bit; they may try something a little different. But if you're still not taking that bait, they're eventually going to go fish somewhere else. If they're not getting the reaction that they used to get out of you, then after a while they'll figure out this isn't working anymore. If your buttons are not working anymore, they'll give up on pushing them after a while. If they keep yanking but you stop lurching, you'll be free of that negative energy. It doesn't mean that they're going to cut you out of their life. They may, in which case you don't need that relationship.

Practice and adjust this Experience as needed as you

move closer to your most challenging relationships. It's worth it to keep going. Be aware that you're aware now. You have a new and different perspective on what's going on in this energy game and why people, including yourself, behave the way they do. This game has been played with the same rules for a very long time. You can continue to play, of course, but now you have the choice of a different path—a path toward kinder and more caring relationships, without the conditions and clingy neediness. You can love, yourself and others, freely and unconditionally, as you move forward on your grand journey called life.

CHAPTER 14

REDUCE CONSTANT COMPARISON AND BE AUTHENTIC
- No More Hiding -

Compare yourself to who you were yesterday,
not to who someone else is today.
—*Dr. Jordan Peterson*

LIKE ALL JOURNEYS, you must travel the first steps before you can traverse the later ones. You have been taking steps to explore who you really are, what you truly want, and how you want to be in your life. All of this has been building toward helping you to uncover your authentic Inner Sage.

Now is the time for you to fully own and appreciate your

authentic self and to let your light shine upon the world around you. No more hiding. No more pretending you haven't changed and grown. No more dimming your authentic self. Your uniqueness is undeniable, and your self-acceptance is unfolding with each knowing step. Every Limiting Box you break apart, even if just a little, allows your Inner Sage to become a stronger part of who you are. You can be blocked from accepting yourself just the way you are by the self-doubt that comes with constantly comparing yourself to others.

CONSTANT COMPARISON

It's easy to get caught up in the game of life that is all about comparison. "Where do I stack up? Am I richer than my neighbor? Do I have a newer car than that person? Do I have a bigger house than that other person? Am I as pretty as . . . ? Am I as thin as . . . ?" We do all this comparison against other people's or society's models of what we think we want to be or don't want to be, have or don't want to have. It's a tiring game, but we do it in our heads all the time, and usually we do it subconsciously. It just goes on and on in the background without us ever checking it. We let it run rampant, unleashed, and untethered until we run neck deep into the mud puddle mentality of "not enough."

We're not good enough. We don't have enough. We have self-doubt and low self-esteem.

This is the negative energy that comes with constant comparison, which is a very Limiting Box in which to find yourself. You're jealous. You're jealous because someone got a raise and you didn't. Or you're envious of somebody because they attained something you want, and they got there before you. We play all these ridiculous games at different levels, and it leads to a sense of competition. It's you against . . . *everybody*.

Comparison and competition go hand in hand. They can impact all areas of your life. Health, wealth, image, relationships, everything. In all of them, the real truth is that you are likely not the best. But you are also not the worst. Your Inner Sage knows this to be true, but if your backseat driver is still in charge of your mind then you will focus on the comparison and competition so it can stay in charge. Does it really matter where you are compared to somebody else?

With very few exceptions, the answer is no. Emphatically no. But if your mind is stuck thinking that it *does* matter, this leads to you thinking you're not good as other people, that there must be something wrong with you. You're not accepting of yourself for who you are and where you are and what you are doing at this time and place in your life. This berating of yourself is all red zone chatter and it most definitely is not helping you. Would you tell a dear friend you cared about deeply that they weren't good enough? Of course you wouldn't. So, don't say it to yourself.

The game of comparing yourself to and competing with others becomes judgmental. Not only do we judge other people's choices, accomplishments, and acquisitions, but we then also judge ourselves as to how we stack up against the ones we are judging. That's a lot of judgment! Do you think all that judgment brings positive or negative energy into your life? Comparison and competition can also lead to grudges against those who gained something bigger than or before you did. Again, do you think that brings positive or negative energy into your life? Judgment and grudges all contribute to the walls of the Limiting Box born of constant comparison. Living life from within this box is exhausting, unhealthy, and heavy.

The game of comparison and competition begins early in life. Parents can, intentionally or unintentionally, start this with siblings. Then school teaches us to be competitive, for grades, praise, and gold stars. It continues into the workplace, as we compete for promotions and raises. It spills into our social circles and groups of friends when we try to one-up one another. Played at its worst, this game can lead some to actively sabotage others. Instead of lifting themselves up, some people try to lower those around them. This is a sad and negative way to go about life which only attracts more negative energy.

Even if you somehow manage to "win" the rat race, you're still a rat. If that is what you aspire to, then great, keep running. But if that doesn't feel in alignment with your authentic self and who you want to be, then consider getting back to living your truth and being your authentic self and not caring so much about what people think of you or where you stack up against them. Strive to be the best version of yourself you can be and make the commitment of being a little bit better each day. That's the competition you want, with yourself.

The good news is that the Limiting Box of constant comparison, competition, and judgment is just that—a box. A box that has been built up over time. You weren't born comparing yourself to others. You picked that up along the way. You can hang onto it, of course, but you can also choose to break the box apart and lessen its weight on your life.

Getting People to Like . . . You?

Since constant comparison with others leads to not feeling you are good enough, you might become—consciously but quite likely unconsciously—more like the people you are comparing yourself against. In an attempt to be and have what they have, you might take on traits or assume behaviors and attitudes you see in other people. This isn't necessarily a bad thing, if your Inner Sage agrees that being this way buttresses your authentic self. If, however, you are becoming someone else in order to get people to accept you or like you, be very careful. You are straying further from your authentic self instead of becoming more aligned with who you truly are. Even if you are successful in getting others to like your assumed persona, it won't be *you* they like, it'll be this pretend version of yourself. You'll have succeeded in getting them to like somebody else.

And how long really can you pretend to be someone you are not? It's draining and understandably so. Your Inner Sage knows this doesn't feel right. You've become more like the people you allowed to make you feel "less than" in the first place. You'll begin to resent yourself more and more if you keep this up. Rita Mae Brown once said, "I think the reward for conformity is that everyone likes you except yourself." Someday, you'll reach a point when you can no longer maintain the masquerade, and when you drop the assumed persona, even if only temporarily, the people you managed to get to like the pretend you will not recognize the real you and those relationships will splinter. Fake friends do not feel fulfilling.

Instead, embrace your uniqueness. Revel in the whole package that is you—your strengths, weaknesses, oddities, and peccadilloes. Instead of judging yourself because you are different than other people, *honor* yourself because you are different than other people. There is no other combination of atoms just like you. Live that; express that; be that. You'll be more peaceful, happier, and have better relationships when you're more authentically you.

Stuck in Reverse

You may be stuck in constant comparison if you feel you are living in a dog-eat-dog world, feeling everyone is out to get you or trying to beat you, that they are "winning" and you are "losing." You may feel you must fight and compete constantly. You don't trust them, and they don't trust you.

Not trusting others and not being trusted is because you've separated yourself from others. Indeed, you feel you must be separated because it's them against you. When you are separated, you can become critical, self-righteous, and prejudiced.

You get to such a place because of judgment. You're

constantly judging others. And you think everyone is judging you because you know you are judging them.

Judgment comes from competing against everyone. Competing against everyone comes from being jealous and wanting what others have. Jealousy comes from constant comparison. It's a classic domino effect.

The walls of your Limiting Box are built from things like judgment, self-righteousness, and prejudice. But the foundation of the wall is constant comparison. It's the keystone. If you can remove the constant comparison, the whole wall comes tumbling down. Ask your Inner Sage if having less of this negative energy feels better for your authentic self.

Experience I: Stop Caring What Other People Think

If we can overcome our fear of being judged, we will increase our capacity for real self-expression and our ability to be our authentic selves, without all the reservations and pretending. Otherwise, as Lao Tzu says, "Care about what other people think and you will always be their prisoner." To stop caring about what other people think is easier said than done, but we are going to give it a try here. You're going to have a little fun with this Experience. Yes, it will have foundational impact on your ability to stop caring what others think of you, so in that sense you absolutely want to make sure you fully live the Experience. But you'll also be able to find some humor in it and laugh at yourself and your swirling thoughts, and at the reactions, both real and imagined, from other people.

- **Go out** in public when you look your worst. Pick a time when you haven't showered all day or for a couple days. A day when you're lying around the house in your worst pair of sweats with the torn seams and the holes in them. Go to the grocery store or the mall like that. Don't change clothes. Don't clean up. Don't comb your hair.

- **Check in** with yourself as you walk around and see if you can stop caring what other people think about you. Observe your thoughts and judgments and comparisons.

- **Remind yourself** you do not know what is going on inside someone else's head, and you do not know for a fact that they are judging you. Recall the quote by Olin Miller, "You probably wouldn't worry about what people think of you if you could know how seldom they do." Ask yourself if you care if complete strangers are judging you. Even if they are, their judgment doesn't physically impact you in the least and it says more about their past and prejudices than it does about you. And since so many people are in the yellow or red zone in their heads, do you really want to take to heart the judgments of a mind that is overcrowded and not thinking clearly? Don't pressure yourself to stop caring what others think on your first try, just keep practicing.

Experience II: What I Like about Me

Many of us tend to be more self-critical than self-aggrandizing. We might be more familiar with our flaws than our strengths. In this Experience, you are going to focus on things you like about yourself, because those are just as important a part of your authentic self.

Write things you like about yourself. Don't limit what you say because you think other people would judge you for it, and don't judge yourself for what you write. Be honest and show some (or heck, a lot) of self-appreciation. Don't feel like you are bragging—if it's true, it isn't bragging. Show yourself some love. When you like yourself more, you'll trust yourself more. Honor your uniqueness. Honor your authenticity.

CHAPTER 15

REDUCE FEELING SEPARATE AND BE CENTERED
– Arrive at the Clearing –

Who do you really think you are?
—Your Inner Sage

YOU ARE NEARING THE END of your journey. The trail may have been rocky, dark, and turbulent, but you've done the hard work along the way and in this penultimate chapter you will emerge from the challenge of the trail calmer and clearer, stronger and wiser. You've come to a place of clear thinking and with an awakened awareness of the immense possibilities of living life not from within the confines of Limiting Boxes, but from the resolute strength of your Power Centers.

We've talked many times about being aware of and checking in with your Inner Sage. You've been doing it in chunks in each chapter to break out of each Limiting Box. This chapter is about you now fully owning a life centered in your Inner Sage and no longer solely checking in with that part of yourself when you think of it. This is about completing the shift to a fully centered life that wholly embodies your Inner Sage and relegates your ego-centered mind to be used when you choose to employ it as the best tool for a given task. This is no longer just an Experience on paper that you have temporarily, and then go back to living life as you've always done. It's time to *live* the Experience, not just *have* the Experience. The roles will be reversed and you will move from living in a state of mind that is detached and separate from others (and, indeed, all the world around you), to living life as your Inner Sage, connected to everyone and everything, and seeing yourself as part of the whole.

Your ego isn't all bad, so you don't want to get rid of it completely. Your ego can help by telling you to look your best for that job interview or first date or to try your best on a project. There's nothing wrong with wanting to be your best. The egoic mind we are talking about is when you overly identify with the labels and praise you've taken on.

An overly inflated ego leads to a sense of separation and detachment if it makes you feel superior or unable to relate to people or situations that are different than what you are accustomed to or prefer. Who defines *overly*? As you probably know by now, *you do.*

Fair warning: This chapter might piss off your ego. If you feel any upset as you make your way through this chapter, or thoughts come up that say this is a bunch of bullshit and you should put the book down and walk away: Notice that, pay attention to that, and know it's the remnants of your ego saying it. Your Inner Sage is being put back in its rightful place in the driver's seat, and the ego won't simply, suddenly, and obediently sit quietly in the backseat. Your ego knows it is losing dominance and it will want to stay in control.

But as you can probably feel, there is no stopping your Inner Sage now. You've uncovered and unleashed the real driver, gotten reacquainted with him, and he's stronger than ever. Now it's time to put him firmly back in the driver's seat.

ROLES, LABELS, AND MASKS
Who do you really think you are?

We are a compilation of a lot of things. We have multiple

roles and identities. We've been assigned multiple labels. We wear many masks. We are a compilation of our thoughts, ideas, and beliefs. We've got our name and education, our skills and strengths, our weaknesses and failures, our family and relationships, worries, desires, fears, comparisons. And on and on and on. All of that makes up who we think we are. And the key word here is *think*.

Your egoic mind loves to identify with your various masks and labels, but you are so much more than any title, role, or persona. You might have taken each on willingly and knowingly, or perhaps you took them on unconsciously or without your consent, or at such a young age that you didn't know any better, or they simply *happened*, slowly but surely over the many years you've spent running on the treadmill of life. However you took them on, know that these are things you *think* you are. And in your mind, they are "yours." You even call them yours when you refer to things as "my job," "my title," "my relationships," "my stuff," and so on. That sense of "my, my, my" builds your ego because it requires your ego to keep track of and build an identity around all these masks and labels.

To fully shift to living life as your Inner Sage, however, you need to ask yourself, "Am I *really* those things? *All* of them?" Ask yourself if you feel you are those things. Not *think* you are, *feel* you are. Now that you've rediscovered your Inner Sage and are listening to it more and more, ask these things of your true self and ignore for a minute the outside world and your own mind. Ask your Inner Sage. *Listen* to your Inner Sage. Think less, feel more.

We all have different identities and traits that we bring out in different situations. For example, you behave and speak differently at work than you do with family or when you are out with friends. Having these various identities isn't a horrible thing, but when you *don't know* you have them or you're *not aware* of when you are wearing them you can unconsciously mistake them for who you truly are, even if they are not altogether in alignment with your true self. This is kicking your Inner Sage out of the driver's seat.

Become aware of how you speak, react, and behave in life's various situations. Imagine you are observing your interactions from nearby as an unbiased third party. Watch yourself. Listen to yourself. Are you being true to your true self, or does the way you are speaking or behaving make you cringe a little inside? Allowing for the necessary differences in your behavior depending on the situation, make sure you are still honoring your Inner Sage. Speak *your* words, not the memorized words of others. Respond in ways that align with who you are instead of reacting as expected or out of uncontrolled emotion. Don't pretend to be something or somebody you are not.

Of course, you still need to function in various aspects of your life. You still need to sometimes play in other people's sandboxes. Just be aware of any compromises you are making as you do so. For your collection of roles, labels, and masks, be aware of the degree to which they are, or are not, in alignment with your Inner Sage. Do they make you weaker or do they strengthen you? When you act from behind them, do you feel you are swimming in quicksand, or do you feel like you are standing on pretty solid ground? How do you feel inside afterward? Is your inner light lessened or is it glowing brighter?

Becoming aware of your various roles, identities, and masks—understanding them and where they came from and when and how you use them, and then, ultimately, bringing them more into alignment with who you truly are—leads to a content simplicity. It's much easier to approach interactions as your true self as opposed to having to spin up an identity that is only a tiny bit you. Constantly changing roles or masks is exhausting. Being yourself isn't draining. *Not being yourself* is draining. Life can be a costume party, and masks, labels, and roles may be required at times. But once you become aware of yours, you won't adopt them unconsciously. You can make a choice—they are absolutely within your sphere of control. You can keep them, modify them, or discard them completely.

You certainly aren't the only one doing this. The world simply functions that way, encouraging and expecting you to become egocentric and "different than." But it's not your natural state. You didn't come into this world feeling separate and disconnected. Your ego built up over time as the world encouraged you to look at others, at "those people," as different and separate and not possibly connected to you in any way. With each chapter you've been breaking apart the Limiting Boxes of chatter that feed the egoic mind and help keep it in charge of so much of your life, so much of the time. You can now default to living life as your Inner Sage instead of as your fragile ego, built upon all your labels and masks.

HOW THE EGO KEEPS YOU UNCENTERED

Extreme Ego

On the extreme side of living from your ego, we can get a sense of self-importance that grows out of control. Some people get very self-centered and selfish. They think they are better than, smarter than, something else than. They think they are more virtuous, moral, or righteous. They think their opinions are right and all other opinions are wrong. They think they know it all and the world would be better if everyone simply thought, believed, and chose as they do.

Guess what? All those "other people" are thinking *the same thing,* and where does that leave all of us? Feeling even more different than and separate from others and making the ego even more defensive and aggressive. The negative energy of division is a very Limiting Box indeed. It is more in alignment with your Inner Sage to be open and aware to the reality that, despite what the leaders of your various groups and the media might say, you have more in common with others than you have differences.

Too much self-importance can also lead to too much seriousness, where *everything* becomes a major life drama and you lose the ability to relax and not take things, especially yourself, so seriously. Do you know any drama kings or drama queens? People who habitually react to every situation with overly emotional performances? Are you one of them? If you don't know anyone in your life like that, you can easily find this drama all over the media. These are people that make a mountain out of every molehill. They take the smallest thing and then, all of a sudden, the sky is falling and the world is coming to an end. And of course, that is rarely the case. Your Inner Sage helps you keep things in perspective. Approaching life as your Inner Sage gives you the wisdom of knowing a molehill is just a molehill, and it doesn't have to become a mountain.

Knowledge versus Wisdom

There's a difference between knowing something and having wisdom. Some people with a weakened or nonexistent Inner Sage become know-it-alls and want to explain everything they know to you. This can flow from an extreme ego. They are living more from their egoic mind, and they want to prove to you that they know, and you don't. They've done all this studying and learning, or worse, they've watched all this mainstream media, and now they want to prove they know it all and tell you all about it. People with such a weakened Inner Sage are not as easily capable of considering the possibility that there might be other answers, other explanations, or other viewpoints. That comes from their ego. If you know anyone like this, or if you are like this, that is coming from an ego that can't withstand being questioned or challenged, when in fact, being challenged is what can lead to expanded learning and the adoption of beliefs that are more in alignment with one's true self, or to help solidify one's previously held beliefs. Don't blindly believe talking heads and know-it-alls. Do your own research. Listen to your Inner Sage. Make up your own mind.

Working Mind

You won't be abandoning your mind. As we've said, your mind is an amazing tool and should be used when it is the best instrument for the task at hand. But your egoic mind won't be the default resource used to approach all life situations. Perhaps a better name for this incredible instrument is your *working mind*. Your Inner Sage knows when your working mind is needed and you will use it to do what it does best, like create spreadsheets, fix the car, and plan your vacation. But you won't identify with it and live from it. You won't approach situations in life, including the situations where your mind is heavily involved, *from* the working mind. You will approach even those "mind things" from your Inner Sage, which means from the natural place of love and kindness, and you will employ your working mind as needed.

Having your Inner Sage be the overall and first approach to all areas of your life means all situations and people, including yourself, will be treated with your Inner Sage's natural love and kindness. Because the egoic mind is no longer in the driver's seat, you will live life with a sense of what is best for everyone in any given situation. You won't live life first from the egoic mind, which tends to see everything as a competition and yourself as separate from all else. You will naturally ask yourself, "What's the best possible thing I can do in this situation, that yields the best possible result for myself and everyone involved?"

This is a much more positive energy Power Center from which to live. People will notice, even if they don't know why. People will want to interact with you more socially, at work, and in play. People will begin to recognize that you are not egocentric or living life just for yourself, that you are not trying to lift yourself up by lowering everyone around you but that you are instead trying to lift everyone up. You will be a magnet for positive opportunities.

HOW DO YOU KNOW?

How do you know if it's your centered Inner Sage or your separate-from-everything egoic mind running things? This is an important distinction, and it may take some practice to discern. After all, just because thoughts are coming from your egoic mind doesn't mean they are evil or should be completely ignored.

Here is a simple way to help you hone your perception. When a situation arises and you are wondering how to respond, tune in to your thoughts. Do they feel loving and kind and peaceful? Do they feel in harmony with the energy of your Power Centers of being safe, content, confident, loving, authentic, or centered? If so, you can trust your Inner Sage is calmly running things. If, however, it feels more like the negative energies of the Limiting Boxes of fear, wanting, worry, neediness, comparison, or separation, then it's your ego trying to control things and stay in charge.

It can be subtle and ineffable, but if your Inner Sage is strong then you'll just *know* how things feel. Your egoic mind, however, will need to *convince* you of how they feel.

Experience: Shedding Roles, Labels, and Masks

This Experience will help you shed the last remaining remnants of any *overly* egoic identification with your roles, labels, and masks. It will also help you identify which of these you wish to become a bigger part of your life and which you don't. The goal of this Experience isn't to do away with any particular part of yourself, but to instead shed light on your roles, identities, and masks so you can decide if you want to keep them, tweak them, or drop them. It is always your choice.

Anytime you can alter your roles, labels, and masks to be

more in alignment with your Inner Sage, you'll naturally feel your Power Center of being centered within yourself. Living less from any egoic mind aspects of your various roles, labels, and masks will mean you feel less separation from life because not everything will be a competition or a comparison. Less separation means a more centered oneness within you.

List the different forms your ego, your roles, and your identities take. Look at the various masks you wear in different situations and environments, the labels you've given yourself over time or others have given you, and the roles you play in different areas of your life. Write them all down. Don't judge them as they come up or try to figure them out yet. Just write them all down. You're likely going to be surprised by just how many labels you have and masks you wear. Perhaps it is best to do this over a few days as you find yourself in various situations in real life, noticing and aware now of any identity or mask you've assumed.

Labels: (ex: procrastinator, good husband, drinker, leader, hero, etc.)

Masks: (ex: the tough mask, the stoic mask, the unhurtable mask)

Roles: (ex: your job title, "father," "brother," etc.)

Review your list one at a time and *think* about how these identities serve you. Then, see how they make you *feel*—go deep with this one by locating your Inner Sage and listening. Ask yourself questions like:

- Where did that come from?

- How old is that?

- Do I still want to *be* that?

- How much of my life do I experience from that role or mask or label?

- Do I still want to do that?

- Are there some I no longer want?

- Or maybe some I just want to diminish a little bit?

- And others I want to expand and grow?

- If it's a role I don't have a choice in, like father or son, how can I be in that role more as my Inner Sage?

Shine your light on each one. Your Sage will do the rest.

CHAPTER 16

REDUCE DESPAIR AND BE FREE
-Begin Your New Adventure -

If you knew how powerful your thoughts are,
you would never think a negative thought.
—*Peace Pilgrim*

CONGRATULATIONS! You've reached what is both the end and a new beginning on your journey. You have traveled far; you've done much work, and you've shown courage through it all. You are on the final leg of your expedition through the rugged terrain of your inner world. You should be proud of yourself.

You are also beginning a new adventure—your life lived in alignment with who you truly are and how you truly wish to be. A life lived as your Inner Sage. A life lived with smaller Limiting Boxes. This is not only a gift to yourself, but a treasure for those around you. We are most proud of you.

Add up all the ideas and ahas in all the chapters of this book and that's where you find yourself. You are in a land of new ideas, new possibilities, a new life, and a new you. We call this final Power Center *free* because that's what you are now—a free being. It's the culmination of stacking all the Power Centers together. You are safe, content, confident, loving, authentic, and centered. That's freedom.

You have lessened the limitations from your fears, desires, worries, neediness, comparisons, and separations. We chose to call the sum of those negative energies despair because when you are weighed down by too much of too many of those, that's what you'll have. You can choose now whether you want to be free or to be limited by despair.

You may find yourself slipping backward toward your Limiting Boxes every now and then. If you do, know that's not uncommon because our brains seek out what is familiar. If living from your Limiting Boxes had become your normal, your mind may seek them out simply because you've carved that deep rut into your neural pathways through repeated use. Now you know you can choose differently.

Do your own math here. What is available to you now

is the pure energy of existence. What some people call living on purpose, or living in the flow, or being present in the *now*. When you live from the positive energies of your Power Centers, you are plugged into the main energy source of all existence. You could say this is living life the way it was meant to be lived—a life divine.

Being free is living in the green zone pretty much all the time, even when the you-know-what hits the fan. It is certainly much freer than living with the exhausting chatter that puts you in the yellow and red zones. Now you have awareness and tools to observe your chatter and make a shift to get back in the driver's seat of life. With a quiet mind under your control, the wheel is back in your hands. You're only one choice away.

Or . . . you can continue with the usual. The same ol', same ol'. Living as an uptight, overwhelmed, short-sighted, narrow-minded, red-zone-headed human is not only tiring for you, it's exhausting to be around. Even if you are only "that guy" some of the time, we've shown you that you don't *need* to be that guy *anytime*. Attempting to keep a lid on all of your Limiting Boxes is a daunting task for even the most committed control freak. Eventually you'll blow a gasket, and that lid will go flying off.

Being free is being in the flow of life. Like when us

Offroad Monks are out crawling over the obstacles of life on the trail, we're always looking for the smoothest path, as if we were water finding the path of least resistance. Being in the flow is easier than fighting your demons while swimming upstream with half your brain tied behind your back while it struggles with justifying and rationalizing your red-zone chatter with yet more red-zone chatter. Whew! It's exhausting just writing that. Imagine for a minute what your life might be like now that you can sense, feel, and *know* that the green zone choices you're making are the smoothest path through life.

Remember, life isn't always going to be boring or slow. The journey will challenge you. There will always be some obstacles to drive over, through, or around, day after day, week after week, year after year until the day you leave the trail for the last time. Take this book with you while you take the wheel of your life with a quiet mind, your feet on the floor, and your ass in the driver's seat.

Experience: Be Free

The Experience for this chapter is simple (and surprise! There's no writing!). But remember, simple does not mean easy. Here is all you need to do:

Go live your new life as your new and rediscovered self.

Every morning, before rising, decide to try for this day to use what you've learned in this book to think differently about yourself, about others and their actions, and about each situation you find yourself in. Your new thoughts will lead to new actions and you'll get new results. It's all well within your sphere of control and you don't need anyone else's permission.

You'll need to *choose* to change your thoughts. You'll need to first be aware that your thinking is heading down a well-worn path that you now wish to try avoiding. You can then choose to try a different path. You can choose, even if it's a bit forced in the beginning, to think differently, and then act differently. You'll need to do this consistently. Once in a great while won't regroove the neural pathways in your mind that you've spent years carving.

We've seen many people have this Experience. We are confident you will, too.

AFTER THOUGHTS

"That's it? Now I'm all better?" Perhaps. But remember, you don't brush your teeth only once in life.

ONGRATULATE YOURSELF for Taking the Wheel. Pat yourself on the back. Give yourself a hug. Do a little dance. But don't go back to being in your life the same way you were beforehand. You chose this book for a reason, so take the parts that speak to you and choose a new path for your way of being present each and every day of your life.

Your introduction to chatter may be ending, but your journey toward your true self is just beginning. Listen to your awakened Inner Sage. Shush your thoughts. You *can* choose differently. You *can* choose to journey through life more aligned and with less noise in your head. The new ways of being which you are taking with you from this book might take awhile before they become your default mode of being on a daily basis. That's okay. As you practice what you have learned, don't aim for perfection. Make your aim over time to first restore your Inner Sage to 51 percent control over your chatter. In the meantime, simply observe yourself and your thinking as you interact with your life. *Pay Attention to Everything.* Tune in to your feelings in trying moments and decide if you want to think and act the way you always have, or if you want to make a shift, however small, in your thoughts and your actions and try something new. Remember, your thoughts lead to your actions which lead to your results. What you think and how you feel *is* what your life becomes, and they are the only things you control. Everyone has long-standing habits, so this won't be an overnight process, but keep going. Your Power Centers are waiting for you.

Now that you have completed the book, take the Perceived Stress Survey in chapter 1 again and add your score to the Chatter Level Chart. You are encouraged to occasionally take the Perceived Stress Survey over the coming months (and the coming years) and each time you do, add your score to the Chatter Level Chart. Your scores might fluctuate up and down, because life has its ups and downs, but over time see if you are moving more toward the green zone. The things you take with you from this book will help you, but only if you do them on a regular basis. This will help you blend them into your new way of being in your life.

A journey on a new path is rarely a simple straight line with clear skies and no potholes. Consider any obstacles you encounter on this path as opportunities to apply what you have learned in this book. Revisit chapters as needed. Let go of your self-centered egoic self a bit and live life more from your Inner Sage. If you apply what you've learned, you'll notice a shift that, while it may seem small at first, will compound and grow, and your life will begin feeling more in alignment with your true self.

In effect, your life will feel more like *your* life.

You'll see other people's words and actions in a new light when you allow for the possibility that they are coming from their own personal Limiting Boxes. As you unhook from some of your life's drama, you'll feel freer and lighter and more connected to yourself and the universe. As you get better at observing your thoughts and choosing different ones, or, on occasion, quieting your mind and not having any thoughts at all, you'll find a peaceful calm. Believe it or not, your clarity can actually improve the fewer thoughts you have. Less clutter with the rehashing of thoughts you've thought a million times, and less time spent on the worry-go-round about the future, means more space for what matters most to you *now* to rise to the surface.

Here's another thing that may happen. You may get an initial burst of clarity in your thoughts and a lightness in your feelings. You may begin to feel more alignment in your life and excitement for your future. But don't be surprised if the crazy drama of life comes rushing back even stronger than before. Society in general, and people in your life in particular, may prefer that you not change, that you go back to behaving and reacting the way you did previously. People will notice that you've made a shift in your life, that you're thinking and acting in new ways, and they may push back, possibly more fiercely than before. If this happens, it doesn't mean your new approach is wrong. If you've decided, and decided from a place of knowing that feels truly in alignment within you, then you can choose how to respond and not simply react to the pushback. This may be one of those things in your life where you take a few steps forward and then a couple of steps back. That's okay. New journeys frequently go that way. Things that are worth doing are simply that, *worth doing*, even if you encounter setbacks.

In addition to others reacting to your shift, be aware that your own ego might come roaring back after you've diminished it, because it rarely wants to give up control easily and willingly. Your egoic mind may tell you this is all a bunch of nonsense, and you should just go back to your old ways because they're familiar, they're easier, and they are what everyone expects of you. Remember that our minds like recognizable patterns and can resist change in the guise of keeping us safe. If you feel a pull to go back to your old ways, try to discern if the reason is simply because it's known. More often than not, the authentic you that has begun to emerge wishes to continue on your new journey.

In his book *The Power of Now*, Eckhart Tolle said, "Your outer journey may contain a million steps; your inner journey only has one: the step you are taking right now." If you feel overwhelmed at times, bring your awareness to the one step you are taking now. One step is much easier than a million steps. One step is doable. Take it, however small. See what happens. Remember the analogy of turning a ship at sea one degree. One step can be your turn. When you are ready, take another step. Try things out. Observe what happens inside you and around you. Have some fun with this. Be curious. Continue practicing what you have chosen to take with you from this book. You will soon be in a much better place within yourself, a place *you* have decided to go. Observe your chatter but know you don't have to obey its every utterance.

Listen to your Inner Sage and it will grow stronger. Continue listening and you'll see that you and your Inner Sage are one and you have wisdom you can trust inside you.

CONTENT NOTE

THIS BOOK DISCUSSES suicide and mental health. If you or someone you know is struggling with thoughts of suicide or is in emotional distress, you can access free and confidential emotional support by calling 988, the National Lifeline. If it is a life-threatening situation, call 911.

You can also contact the Substance Abuse and Mental Health Services Administration (SAMHSA) National Helpline at 1-800-622-HELP (4357) to access free, confidential referral and information services for individuals and families facing mental health and/or substance use challenges.

OUR GRATITUDES

THE INFORMATION IN THIS BOOK is a compilation of wisdom, teachings, and tips from great sages past and present. We provide their names here to express our humble and profound gratitude for each and every one of them, and for each and every thing we learned from them, whether it's what we wanted to hear at the time or not. We also provide this list for you, the cherished reader, in the event you wish to dig deeper into any of them as you journey toward your own enlightenment.

Albert Einstein

The Buddha

Carl Jung

Carl Rogers

Carlos Castaneda

Dalai Lama

Dan Brown

Dan Millman

Daniel Quinn

David Bowie

David Byrne

Deva Premal

Dolores Cannon

Don Miguel Ruiz

Eckhart Tolle

Esther Hicks

Friedrich Nietzsche

G.K. Gyatso

Gary Zukuv

George Harrison

The Gnostic Christians

Hermann Hesse

James Hollis

James Redfield

James Twyman

Jeff Cavaliere

Jesus Christ

Jill Bolte Taylor

Jim Carrey

John Lennon

Jon Kabat-Zinn

Dr. Jordan Peterson

Kahlil Gibran

Kati Morton

Krishna Das

Kristen Richardson

Leo Hartong

Martin Luther King Jr.

Mel Robbins

Mihaly Csikszentmihalyi

Nelson Mandela

Oprah Winfrey

Paramahansa Yogananda

Pete Walker

Pink Floyd

Ram Dass

Richard Bach

Shunryu Suzuki

Sigmund Freud

Sri Ramakrishna

Swami Sarvapriyananda

Tears for Fears

Theodor Geisel

Tony Horton

The Wachowskis

Dr. Wayne Dyer

XTC

TOMMY

In addition to each of these great sages and teachers, literally everyone and everything in my life has led me to this moment. I guess this is what they mean by "life is your teacher." And while I can't list all I'm grateful to and for, I will call out the one man who was man enough to bring this compilation of sage wisdom to humankind . . . my buddy, Bryan. And the woman by my side, Suma, who graciously put up with being the test student through fifteen years of curriculum development. I wish everyone could experience such love, patience, and constant forgiveness. I am very fortunate to be surrounded by immense and unwavering love, intelligence, and support.

BRYAN

I want to express much gratitude to the many teachers from whom I've learned much of what is in this book. In a way, it wasn't really written by us. It feels more true to say we are simply passing along information and wisdom shared by ancients and currents alike. I'm grateful for them all.

I'm grateful for the difficult times in my life because—while they felt horrible at the time—when I finally came to understand their lessons, I knew that I had to experience them to get to where I am today. I'm grateful for where I am today. I'm content with who I am, having rediscovered my own Inner Sage.

I'm grateful to you, the reader, for having opened this book, and my wish is that it helps you on your journey. If it does, I hope that you'll share it with others.

I'm grateful for Lisa being such a powerful force and source of positive energy in my life. You've helped me grow in innumerable ways, and I couldn't have written this book without you, Beautiful. I'm grateful for Stacy, who's always been unconditionally in my corner. I'm grateful for my boys, whom I love beyond belief and more than anything in this world. I'm most grateful to my mom, who did the best thing a mom can do for a child: Love the hell out of them. Last, I'm grateful for Tommy. I wouldn't be here if not for him. He never gave up on me, even when I had, and he always had a tow strap to pull me forward. I've learned much from you, and I love you, my brother.

Photo of Bryan by James Damian

ABOUT THE AUTHORS

B ryan Bernard's and Tommy Stoffel's Soul Outing wilderness workshops and expeditions offered through Zen 4-Wheeling help diverse groups calm stress and reduce inner chatter to help people make fundamental, lasting improvements in their lives. The authors are cohosts and executive producers of the *Offroad Monks* documentary. Bryan is a seeker; Tommy, a peace bringer.